Houghton Mifflin
Reading

Adventures

Senior Authors
J. David Cooper
John J. Pikulski

Authors
David J. Chard
Gilbert Garcia
Claude Goldenberg
Phyllis Hunter
Marjorie Y. Lipson
Shane Templeton
Sheila Valencia
MaryEllen Vogt

Consultants
Linda H. Butler
Linnea C. Ehri
Carla Ford

 HOUGHTON MIFFLIN   BOSTON

Acknowledgments begin on page 427.

Printed in the U.S.A.

ISBN: 0-618-61936-4

2 3 4 5 6 7 8 9 10 DOW 11 10 09 08 07 06

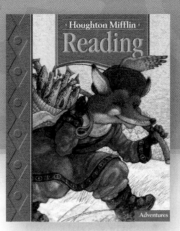

Adventures

Theme 1: Silly Stories 10

Focus on *Poetry* 110

Theme 2: Nature Walk 124

Focus on *Fables* 240

Theme 3: Around Town:
Neighborhood and Community 254

Glossary 416

Theme 1

Silly Stories

◀ Theme Connections ▶

Silly Stories with Wong Herbert Yee **10**

Background and Vocabulary **16**

Fantasy

Shopping *from* **Dragon Gets By** **18**
written and illustrated by Dav Pilkey
Strategy Focus: Summarize

Science Link: Roly Poly **34**
Skill: How to Follow Directions

Student Writing Model ▶ **A Story** **38**

Background and Vocabulary **40**

Fantasy

Julius **42**
by Angela Johnson, illustrated by Dav Pilkey
Strategy Focus: Monitor and Clarify

Social Studies Link: It's Easy to Be Polite **64**
Skill: How to Scan for Information

Fantasy

Background and Vocabulary...........................68

Mrs. Brown Went to Town...........70

written and illustrated by Wong Herbert Yee

Strategy Focus: Predict and Infer

Language Arts Link: Oodles of Riddles 92

Skill: How to Read a Riddle

Theme Wrap-Up

Check Your Progress

Fantasy

Read and Compare 94

The Surprise *from* **George and Martha Round and Round**.................................96

written and illustrated by James Marshall

Nonfiction

Hippos 104

by Claire Miller

Think and Compare 107

Taking Tests **Choosing the Best Answer**..........108

POETRY

Poetry 110

People 113
by Charlotte Zolotow

Covers 113
by Nikki Giovanni

Why Is It? 114
written by Shel Silverstein

Migration/Migración 115
by Alma Flor Ada

The Camel 116
by Langston Hughes

The Gecko 116
by Douglas Florian

**There was a sad pig
with a tail** 117
by Arnold Lobel

The Pickety Fence 118
by David McCord

Fish 119
by Mary Ann Hoberman

I Like It When It's Mizzly 120
by Aileen Fisher

Wind/Viento 121
by Francisco X. Alarcón

Rest here 121
by Issa

NATURE WALK

Theme Connections

Nature Walk with Jane Yolen **124**

Background and Vocabulary **130**

Realistic Fiction

Henry and Mudge and the Starry Night **132**
by Cynthia Rylant, illustrated by Suçie Stevenson
Strategy Focus: Question

Social Studies Link: Campfire Games **160**
Skill: How to Read Instructions

Student Writing Model ▶ **A Description** **164**

Background and Vocabulary **166**

Nonfiction

Exploring Parks with Ranger Dockett **168**
by Alice K. Flanagan, photographs by Christine Osinski
Strategy Focus: Evaluate

Poetry Link: Nature Poems **186**
Skill: How to Read a Poem

NATURE WALK

Realistic Fiction

Background and Vocabulary **188**

Around the Pond:
Who's Been Here? **190**

👤 *written and illustrated by Lindsay Barrett George*
🎀 **Strategy Focus:** Monitor and Clarify

Science Link: How to Be a Wildlife Spy **216**
Skill: How to Read a Science Article

Theme Wrap-Up
Check Your Progress

Realistic Fiction

Read and Compare **220**
Owl Moon **222**
👤 *by Jane Yolen*
illustrated by John Schoenherr

Nonfiction

Owls **235**
by Michael George

Think and Compare **237**

✓ **Taking Tests** **Filling in the Blank** **238**

Focus on Genre

FABLES

Fables 240

**The Hare and
the Tortoise** 242

**The Crow and
the Pitcher** 244

**The Grasshopper
and the Ants** 246

Belling the Cat 248

**The Fly on
the Wagon** 250

Around Town
Neighborhood and Community

Theme Connections

Around Town with Gary Soto 254

Background and Vocabulary 260

Realistic Fiction

Chinatown 262
written and illustrated by William Low
Strategy Focus: Summarize

Math Link: Make a Tangram 288
Skill: How to Read a Diagram

Student Writing Model ▶ A Friendly Letter 292

Background and Vocabulary 294

Nonfiction

A Trip to the Firehouse 296
by Wendy C. Lewison
photographs by Elizabeth Hathon
Strategy Focus: Question

Health Link: Fire-Safety Tips 320
Skill: How to Take Notes

Realistic Fiction

Background and Vocabulary **324**

Big Bushy Mustache **326**

by Gary Soto, illustrated by Joe Cepeda
Strategy Focus: Predict and Infer

Poetry Link: Family Poems **360**
Skill: How to Read a Poem

Realistic Fiction

Background and Vocabulary **364**

Jamaica Louise James **366**

by Amy Hest, illustrated by Sheila White Samton
Strategy Focus: Evaluate

Art Link: Sidewalk Sticks **394**
Skill: How to Follow a Recipe

Theme Wrap-Up
Check Your Progress

Realistic Fiction

Read and Compare **396**

Grandpa's Corner Store **398**

written and illustrated by DyAnne DiSalvo-Ryan

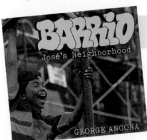

Nonfiction

Barrio: *José's Neighborhood* **409**

written and photographed by George Ancona

Think and Compare **413**

Taking Tests Writing a Personal Response **414**

Glossary **416**

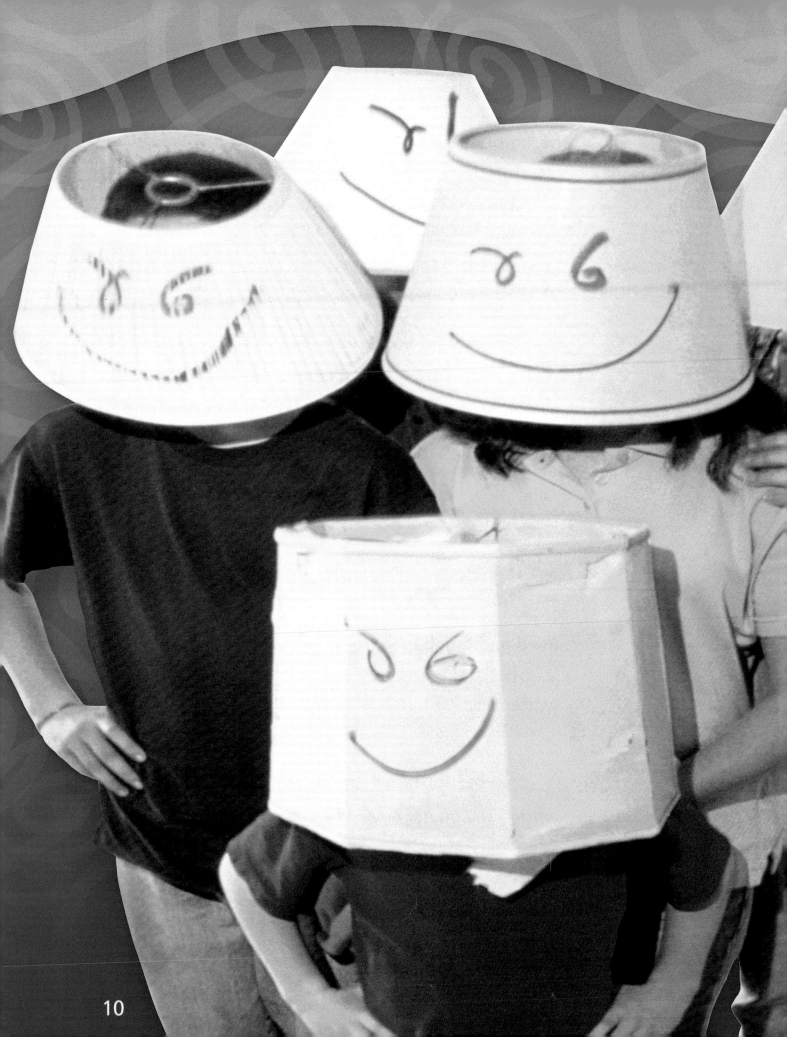

Silly Stories

Smile

It takes a lot of work to frown.

It's easier to smile —

Just take the corners of your mouth

And stretch them for a mile.

by Douglas Florian

Silly Stories

with Wong Herbert Yee

You can use a recipe to make a
mountain of chocolate chip cookies,
stacks of pancakes, or even a story.
Here is a recipe for a silly story from
Wong Herbert Yee. It's sure
to make you smile!

Hi Boys and Girls,

What makes a story silly? First, you need a place, like a farm. Next, you need some things you might find on the farm.

farmer	**farm house**	**straw hat**	**cow**
barn	**overalls**	**kitchen**	**pig**
duck	**pitchfork**	**bucket**	**milk**

Now let's do some mixing.

1. Take the farmer, the barn, the cow, the bucket, and the milk.

2. Put them in a story.

3. Stir them together.

What have you got? You've got a farmer in the barn milking a cow. Wait a minute! What's so silly about that? Farmers milk their cows every day — BORING! Let's try again.

1. Take the cow, the pig, the duck, the straw hat, the pitchfork, and the kitchen.

2. Dump them all in a story.

3. Shake them till you giggle.

What have you got? You've got the cow in the kitchen cooking hot dogs on the pitchfork. You've got the duck dancing on the straw hat, while the pig juggles eggs! That sounds like a recipe for a silly story!

As you read each silly story in this theme, think about what went into the recipe!

Wong Herbert Yee

Giggle at Silly Stories

Wong Herbert Yee has a recipe for a silly farm story. What story could you tell with the same ingredients?

You are about to read some silly stories in this theme. Find out which selection makes you smile the most!

Mrs. Brown Went to Town
by Wong Herbert Yee

JULIUS
Story by Angela Johnson
Pictures by Dav Pilkey

Hippos
Ranger Rick
by Claire Miller

GEORGE AND MARTHA ROUND AND ROUND
JAMES MARSHALL

DRAGON Gets By
Dav Pilkey

Internet

To learn about the authors in this theme, visit Education Place. **www.eduplace.com/kids**

Dragon Gets By

Genre Fantasy

Key Vocabulary

balanced

dairy

diet

hungry

shopping

vegetable

Vocabulary Reader

e ● Glossary

A Balanced Diet

You are going to read a story about a character named Dragon. Dragon does not have a good **diet**. To have a **balanced** diet, he should carefully choose foods from among the different food groups below.

The next time you go food **shopping**, look for the food groups shown. Be sure not to choose too many foods from the last group.

Now, doesn't looking at all of this good food make you **hungry**?

dairy
group

vegetable
group

fruit
group

bread and cereal group

meat, poultry, and nuts group

fats, oils, and sweets group

DRAGON Gets By

Dav Pilkey

Strategy Focus

Dragon's shopping trip turns out to be an adventure. As you read, stop now and then to **summarize**.

Shopping

Dragon looked in his cupboard, but there was no food at all. "The cupboard is bare," said Dragon. "Time to go shopping."

Dragon got into his car and drove. The food store was at the top of a hill. It was a very steep drive.

Dragon loved to go shopping. He was a very wise shopper.

He bought food only from the five basic food groups: He bought cheese curls from the dairy group. He bought doughnuts from the bread group.

He bought catsup from the fruits and vegetables group. He bought pork rinds from the meat group.

And he bought fudge pops from the chocolate group.

Dragon had a balanced diet.

He had so much food that he could not fit it all into his car.

"I know what I will do," said Dragon. "I will eat some of the food now, and then the rest will fit in the car."

Dragon sat in the parking lot and started to eat. He crunched up the cheese curls. He downed the doughnuts. He packed away the pork rinds.

Dragon ate and ate and ate until all the food was gone.

"Burp!"

Now *Dragon* could not fit into his car.
"Oh, what am I going to do?" cried Dragon.
He thought and thought, and scratched his big head.

"I know what I will do," said Dragon. "I will push my car home."

So Dragon pushed his car down the hill. The car began to roll faster and faster . . .

and faster . . .

and faster.

Finally, Dragon's car came to a stop
right in front of his house.

28

All the excitement had made
Dragon very hungry.

He went into his kitchen and looked in the
cupboard. There was no food at all.
"The cupboard is bare," said Dragon.
"Time to go shopping."

Meet the Author and Illustrator

Dav Pilkey

Dav Pilkey is often asked why he spells his name "Dav" instead of "Dave." When Mr. Pilkey was seventeen, he was a waiter at a pizza place. He had to wear a name tag, but the label-maker was broken. Instead of printing "Dave," it printed "Dav" — and the name stuck.

Mr. Pilkey writes and illustrates his own books. He also reads a lot of children's books by other authors. His favorite authors are James Marshall, Arnold Lobel, Dr. Seuss, and Cynthia Rylant.

Other books by Dav Pilkey:

A Friend for Dragon, Dogzilla, The Paperboy

Internet

If you want to find out more about Dav Pilkey, visit Education Place.

www.eduplace.com/kids

Responding

Think About the Selection

1. Think of some helpful tips you could give Dragon next time he goes food shopping.

2. Why do you think Dragon didn't stop eating until all the food was gone?

3. Dragon ate all of the food he couldn't fit in his car. What would you do if you could not fit all of your food in the car?

4. Why do you think Dragon loved to go shopping? How do you feel about shopping?

5. **Connecting/Comparing** What do you think are the silliest parts of this story?

Informing

Write a Shopping List

Make two lists. On the first list, write the names of the foods Dragon bought at the food store. On the second list, write the names of foods you would buy at a food store.

Tips

- **Fold your paper in half as shown.**
- **Number your lists.**

Plan a Balanced Lunch

Make a menu for a balanced lunch. Pick food from the different food groups shown on pages 16–17. Name the food group each item comes from.

Make a TV Commercial

If Dragon were making a TV commercial for his favorite food, what would he say? Plan a commercial. Act it out for your class.

Tips

- **Watch real TV commercials for ideas.**
- **Use describing words, such as *delicious* and *nutritious.***

Internet

Take an Online Poll

What are your favorite foods? Do you like to go shopping? Take the Education Place online poll and tell us. **www.eduplace.com/kids**

Genre

Directions

Skill: How to Follow Directions

❶ Read the title.

❷ Read all of the directions first.

❸ Be sure to gather all of the materials before you begin the activity.

❹ If there are steps to follow, reread each step carefully. Do the steps in order, following the numbers.

Roly-Poly

by Janice VanCleave

I wonder . . . Why do things roll downhill?

Let's find out!

Round up these things:

- ✔ baby powder
- ✔ cookie sheet
- ✔ coffee can
- ✔ masking tape
- ✔ ¼ cup tap water
- ✔ red food coloring
- ✔ coffee cup
- ✔ spoon
- ✔ eyedropper

1. Spread a thin layer of baby powder over the surface of the cookie sheet.

 2. Place the cookie sheet on the floor.

 3. Raise one end of the cookie sheet and rest it on the rim of the coffee can.

 4. Secure the cookie sheet to the can with tape.

5. Put the water and 10 drops of food coloring in the cup. Stir.

 6. Fill the eyedropper with colored water.

 7. Practice squeezing drops of colored water back into the cup until you can easily squeeze one drop at a time.

 8. Sit next to the raised end of the powdered cookie sheet. Hold the eyedropper just above the raised end of the cookie sheet.

9. Squeeze out 1 drop of colored water and watch it roll down the powdered cookie sheet. It will become covered with powder and form a round rolling object that we'll call a roly-poly.

So now we know ...

Gravity is the force that makes things fall to the ground. It also makes round things such as balls and bike wheels roll downhill. That is why your roly-poly rolled down the cookie sheet.

A Story

A story tells about something that is made-up. It has a main character, a beginning, a middle, and an end. Use this student's writing as a model when you write a story of your own.

> Be sure your **title** makes the reader want to read your story.

> The **beginning** of a story tells when and where it takes place.

> Help the reader picture the main **character**. Give details.

The Hungry Panther

On Monday after school, I sat down at my desk. I wanted to finish my drawing of a panther. I got out my purple, black, and blue markers and started to color. Just then, I noticed my panther blink. Or did it? I got scared and ran to tell my mom. She gave me that look. I felt as if she didn't believe me.

That night, I heard a noise downstairs. I got my dad's metal baseball bat from the closet and went downstairs. I saw a blue, black, and purple shape. Then I knew. It was my panther causing the noise. He was in the kitchen making a turkey sandwich!

My panther looked at me and asked, "Do you know where the mustard is?" I was so shocked that I went to my room and got dressed.

My panther and I walked to the ice-cream store. He ate three scoops of vanilla. I ate two scoops of bubble-gum ice cream. On the way home I fell asleep on the panther's back.

The next morning I woke up. I was already dressed for school. My mouth tasted like bubble-gum ice cream. Could this happen to you? Did this really happen to me?

Dialogue makes characters come alive.

The **middle** of a story tells the main events.

The **ending** brings the story to a close. It can surprise you.

Meet the Author

Ashley C.

Grade: two
State: New York
Hobbies: swimming, riding her bike
What she'd like to be when she grows up: a veterinarian

Julius

Genre **Fantasy**

Key Vocabulary

crumbs

imitation

noise

slurped

spread

Vocabulary Reader

Pigs

 ● **Glossary**

40

How Real Pigs Act

What does it mean to act like a pig? Have you ever seen anyone do an imitation of a pig? Do you think that's how pigs really act? In the next story, you'll meet a pig that acts more like a person!

These little piggies **slurped** their food.

Real pigs sometimes **spread** their food out and make messes while they eat.

Real pigs will eat **crumbs** and leftover food, but only if that's what they're fed.

Real pigs make a **noise** called a grunt.

Grunt!

41

Meet the Author
Angela Johnson

Born: June 18 in Tuskegee, Alabama

Where she lives now: Kent, Ohio

Hobbies: Watching old movies, gardening, traveling

When she began writing: "I started writing when I was nine. My parents bought me a diary. I wrote in it every day, mostly about my friends."

Other books: *The Leaving Morning, The Rolling Store, One of Three*

Meet the Illustrator
Dav Pilkey

Born: March 4 in Cleveland, Ohio

Where he lives now: Eugene, Oregon

Pets: He owns three dogs and one cat.

He once had three mice named Rabies, Flash, and Dwayne, but he had to give them away when he moved to Oregon.

Internet

To find out more about Angela Johnson and Dav Pilkey, visit Education Place.

www.eduplace.com/kids

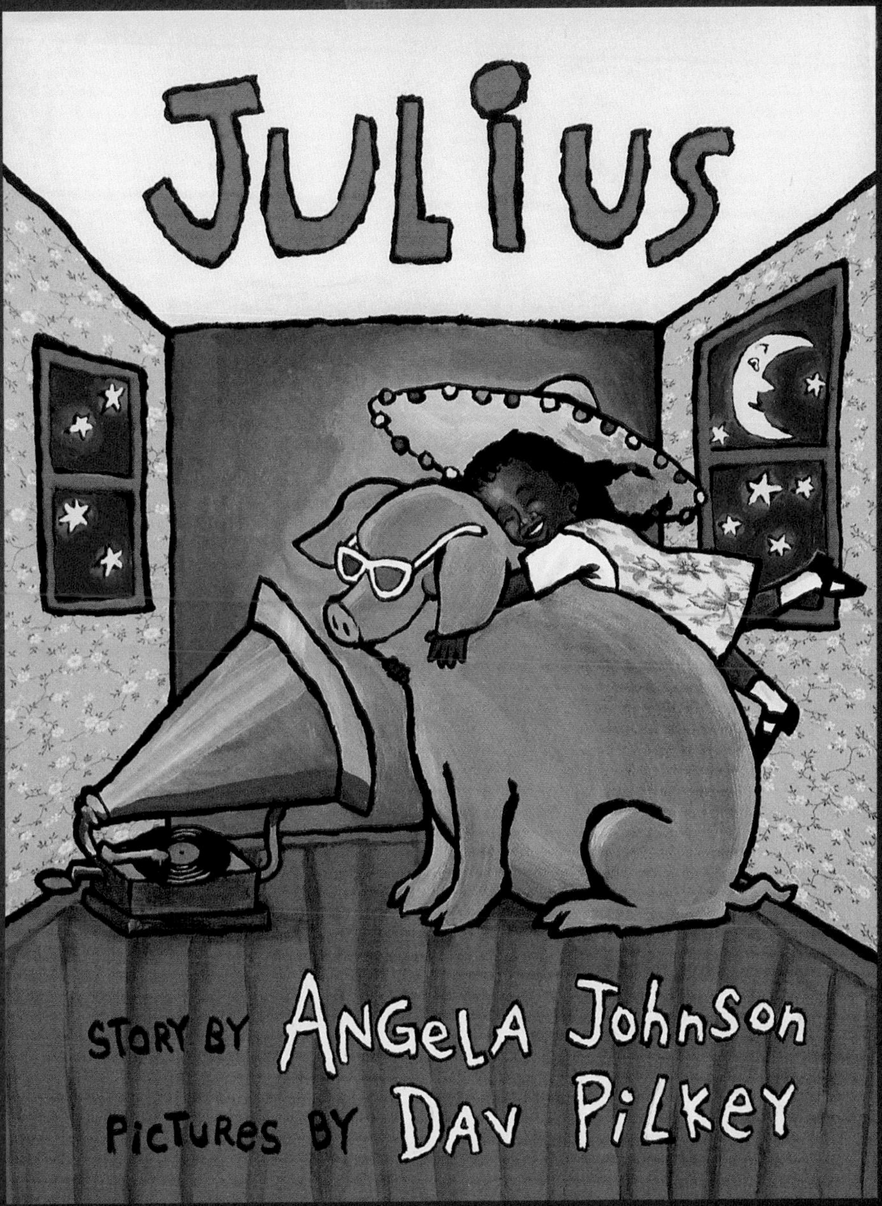

Julius

STORY BY Angela Johnson

PICTURES BY Dav Pilkey

Strategy Focus

While you read about Maya and Julius, **monitor** how well you understand the story. If you're not sure about something, reread or read ahead to **clarify**.

Maya's granddaddy lived in Alabama, but
wintered in Alaska.

He told Maya that was the reason he liked ice
cubes in his coffee.

On one of Granddaddy's visits from Alaska, he brought a crate.

A surprise for Maya!

"Something that will teach you fun and sharing." Granddaddy smiled. "Something for my special you."

Maya hoped it was a horse or an older brother.
She'd always wanted one or the other.

But it was a pig.

A big pig.

An Alaskan pig, who did a polar bear imitation and climbed out of the crate.

Julius had come.

Maya's parents didn't think that they would like
Julius. He showed them no fun, no sharing.
Maya loved Julius, though, so he stayed.

There never was enough food in the house after Julius came to stay.

He slurped coffee and ate too much peanut butter.

He would roll himself in flour when he wanted Maya to bake him cookies.

Julius made big messes and spread the newspaper everywhere before anyone could read it. He left crumbs on the sheets and never picked up his towels.

Julius made too much noise. He'd stay up late watching old movies, and he'd always play records when everybody else wanted to read.

But Maya knew the other Julius, too. . . .

The Julius who was fun to take on walks 'cause he
did great dog imitations and chased cats.

51

The Julius who sneaked into stores with her and tried on clothes. Julius liked anything blue and stretchy.

They'd try on hats too. Maya liked red felt. Julius liked straw — it tasted better.

Trying on shoes was hard, though. . . .

Julius would swing for hours on the
playground with Maya.

He'd protect her from the scary things at night
too . . . sometimes.

Maya loved the Julius who taught her how to dance to jazz records and eat peanut butter from the jar, without getting any on the ceiling.

Maya didn't think all the older brothers in the world could have taught her that.

Julius loved the Maya who taught him that even though he was a pig he didn't have to act like he lived in a barn.

Julius didn't think all the Alaskan pigs in the world could have taught him that.

Maya shared the things she'd learned from Julius
with her friends.

Swinging . . .

trying on hats, and dancing to jazz records.

Julius shared the things Maya had taught him with
her parents . . . sometimes.

Use a Map or Globe

Find the United States on a map or globe.

- In which state does Granddaddy live? Point it out.

- In which state does Granddaddy spend the winter?

Bonus When Granddaddy goes home for the winter, in which direction does he travel? Explain your answer.

Compare Pictures

Dav Pilkey drew the pictures for *Dragon Gets By* and *Julius*. With a partner, look at both stories and discuss the pictures.

Tips

- Use two books. Open one to *Julius*. Open the other to *Dragon Gets By*.
- Compare colors, shapes, and backgrounds.

Internet

E-mail a Friend

What did you like best about *Julius*? Would you tell a friend to read it? Send an e-mail to a friend. Tell your friend about the story.

Genre

Procedures

Skill: How to Scan for Information

❶ Quickly look the page over to find the **title, headings,** and **captions.** Don't read every word.

❷ Identify **key words** and important information.

❸ When you find the information you need, go back and read carefully.

It's Easy to Be Polite
(Why Manners Are Important)

by Beth Brainard and Sheila Behr

The key to being polite is to live by the Golden Rule — treat all people the way you would like them to treat you.

SOUP SHOULD BE SEEN, NOT HEARD!
THE KIDS ETIQUETTE BOOK
By the authors of YOU CAN'T SELL YOUR BROTHER AT THE GARAGE SALE
SLURP! SLURP! SLURP!
BY BETH BRAINARD AND SHEILA BEHR
NEW AND IMPROVED
A COMPLETE MANNERS BOOK FOR CHILDREN

The Magic Words

Thank you!

You're welcome.

Make sure you use the Magic Words every day:

Please
Thank you
You're welcome
Excuse me

Telephone Etiquette

"Hey, Mom, it's for you!"

Hello, this is Suzi.
May I please speak to Ashley?

When you make a call:

- Say *hello*.

- Give your name.

- Ask for the person you're calling. If the person is not there, leave a message or say, *thank you* and *good-bye*. Then hang up. (Always say *good-bye* before hanging up.)

- If you dial a wrong number, say *I'm sorry* and *good-bye*. Then hang up.

When you answer the phone:

Mom, there's a phone call for you.

- Say *hello*.

- If the caller does not give his or her name, say, "May I ask who's calling?"

- Do not giggle or act silly.

- Never stand by the phone and shout. It is always a good idea to go find the person who is wanted on the phone.

When "Call Waiting" signals:

Excuse me for just a moment, Ashley. I'll be right back.

Hello . . . T. J., I'm on the other line. May I call you right back? Thank you. Good-bye.

When leaving a message:

"...at the tone it's a good idea to leave a proper message. BEEP!"

Hello, this is T. J. Jones. I'm calling Suzi. Please call me when you get home. My number is 555-4321. Good-bye.

(T. J. knows how to leave a good message.)

Here are some Phone Tips:

- ◉ Speak clearly.

- ◉ Always use the Magic Words.

- ◉ Do not eat, drink, or chew gum while talking.

- ◉ Always say *good-bye* before hanging up.

- ◉ When someone else is on the line, don't listen. Wait your turn.

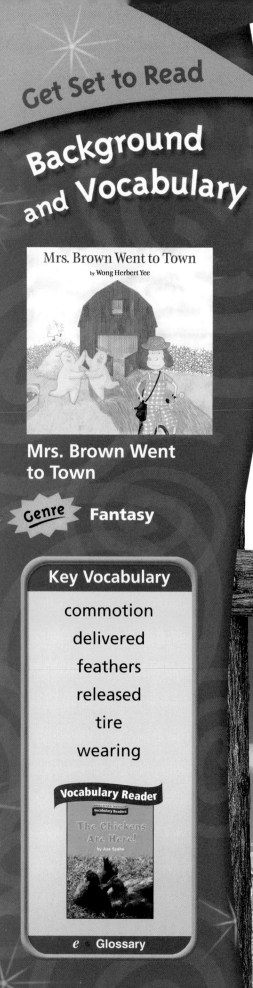

Mrs. Brown Went to Town
by Wong Herbert Yee

Mrs. Brown Went to Town

Genre Fantasy

Key Vocabulary

commotion
delivered
feathers
released
tire
wearing

Vocabulary Reader
HOUGHTON MIFFLIN
Vocabulary Readers
The Chickens Are Here!
by Asa Spahn

e Glossary

Life on a Farm

The story you are about to read takes place on a make-believe farm. Life on a real farm is busy. There's a lot of work to do before food from a farm can be **delivered** to stores and markets.

Each morning, cows are **released** into the fields. At night, they return to their barns.

68

You may see farmers **wearing** gloves or boots. Farm work can be messy.

Feathers fly when it's feeding time in the chicken coop. What a **commotion**!

After a long day, farmers begin to **tire**. They know it's important to rest, because tomorrow will be another busy day.

69

Meet the Author and Illustrator

Wong Herbert Yee

"My advice to people starting out is that being an artist is not something you do. It's what you are. So stick with it! Find a way."

Fact File

- Wong Herbert Yee was born in Detroit, Michigan.
- He now lives in Troy, Michigan.
- His birthday is August 19.
- He has a wife, Judy, and a daughter, Ellen.
- His hobbies include running and bicycling.
- Mr. Yee remembers wanting to be an artist in first grade. "I can still picture my teacher tacking my drawing of a horse with feedbag on the bulletin board. A proud moment."

Other books by Wong Herbert Yee:

Fireman Small to the Rescue; EEK! There's a Mouse in the House; A Drop of Rain

Internet

To find out more about Wong Herbert Yee, visit Education Place.

www.eduplace.com/kids

Mrs. Brown Went to Town

by Wong Herbert Yee

Strategy Focus

Use what you know about animals and make-believe to **predict** what might happen on the farm when Mrs. Brown goes to town.

Mrs. Brown lives in the barn out back
With a cow, two pigs, three ducks, and a yak.
Life on the farm wasn't always this way.
Everything changed just last Saturday.

When riding her bicycle down the street,
A terrier tasted Mrs. Brown's feet.

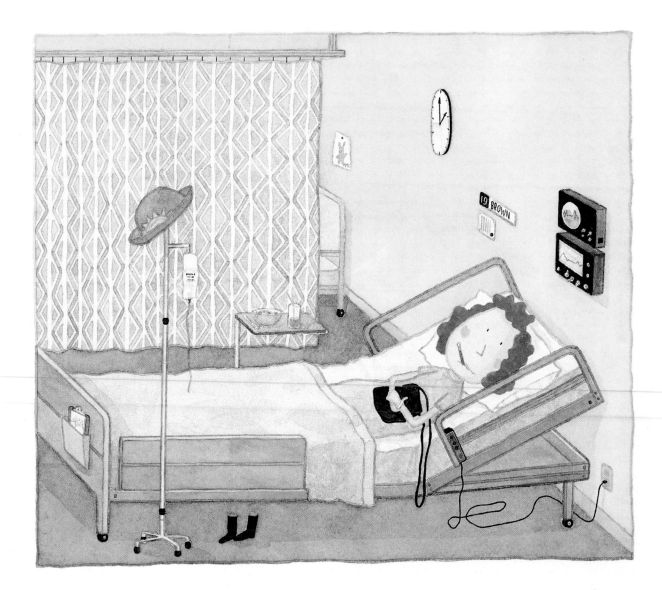

In a hospital bed she rested,
Waiting to be x-rayed and tested.
Mrs. Brown sent word in a letter
To say she'd come home, when she was better.

The postman delivered the letter out back
For a cow, two pigs, three ducks, and a yak.
All the animals, except for a mouse,
Voted to move into Mrs. Brown's house.

They rang the doorbell
To hear the chimes,

Flushed the toilet
One hundred times,

Raced up the stairs, came sliding back down,
Each one wearing a different gown,

Took turns bouncing on Mrs. Brown's bed,

Painted the house in matching barn red.

They raided the pantry,
Prepared a snack
For a cow, two pigs,
Three ducks, and a yak.

In the bathroom they played for hours
Putting on makeup and taking long showers.

They dried off in front of a roaring fire,
Warm and cozy but beginning to tire,
Tiptoed upstairs by candlelight,
Borrowed pajamas to wear for the night.

The hospital released Mrs. Brown at eight.
A taxicab dropped her off by the gate.

She hobbled upstairs and crawled in the sack
Didn't see a cow, two pigs, three ducks, and a yak.

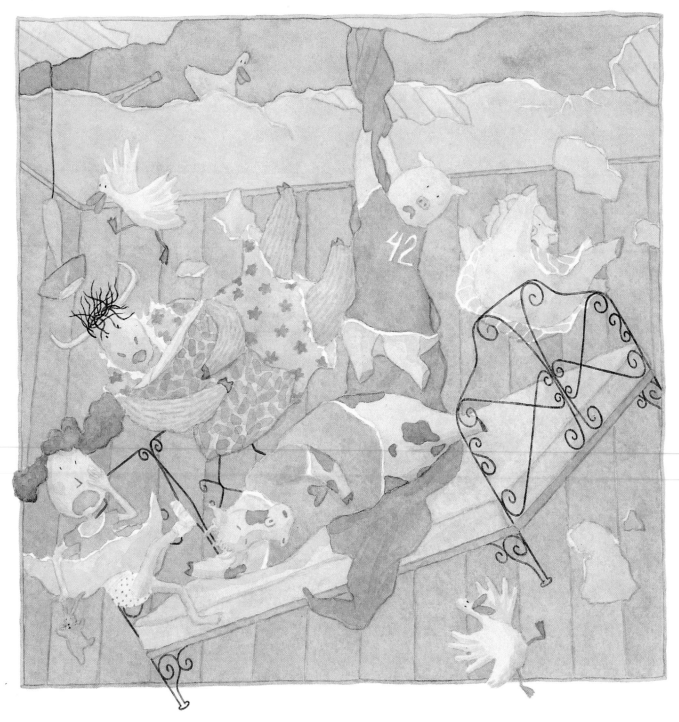

The floor beneath them began to quake.
The walls and windows started to shake.
All this commotion woke Mrs. Brown
In time to feel her bed crashing down!

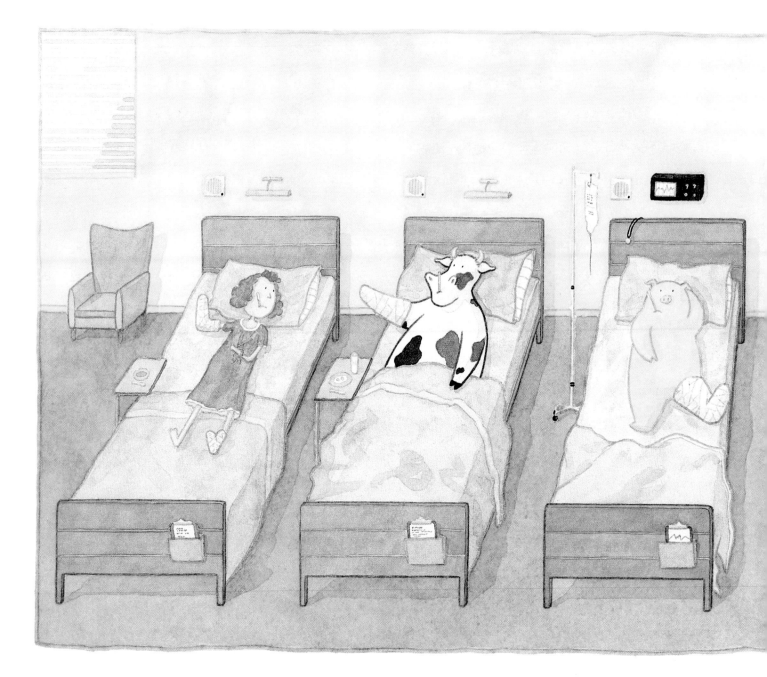

The police were first to arrive on the scene.
Fire trucks dispatched from station thirteen.
An ambulance raced all the way from town
And carried away poor Mrs. Brown.

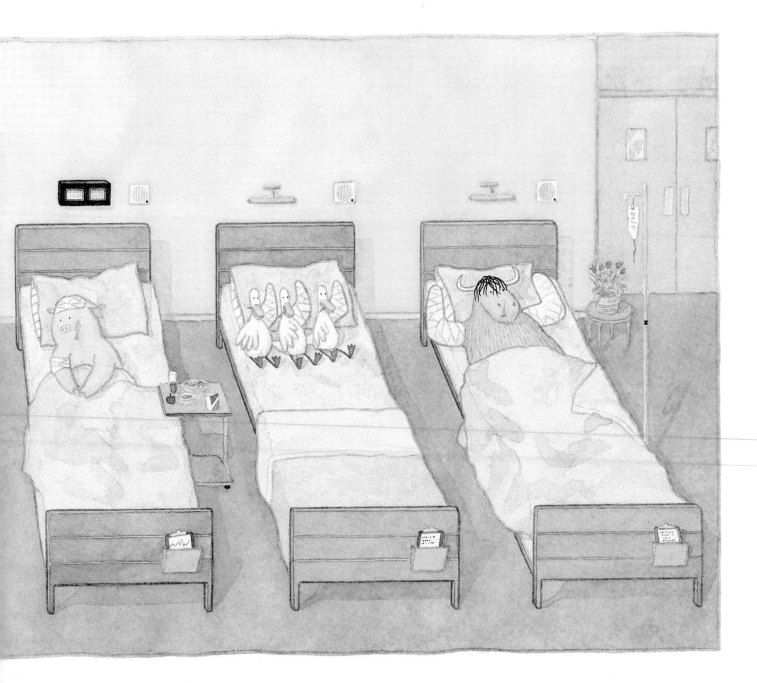

In the hospital she lay on her back
With a cow, two pigs, three ducks, and a yak.
The hospital released Mrs. Brown at ten.
The doctors waved good-bye once again.

Into a taxi they crammed all eight.
The driver dropped them off by the gate.
He swept out the feathers and hair
And charged Mrs. Brown twice the fare.

Life on the farm wasn't always this way
Until Mrs. Brown went to town that day.
So now she lives in the barn out back
With a cow, two pigs, three ducks, and a yak.

Mrs. Brown Went to Town
by Wong Herbert Yee

Think About the Selection

1. Why do you think the animals wanted to move into Mrs. Brown's house?

2. Why didn't the mouse want to move into the house with the other animals?

3. How does Wong Herbert Yee make this story funny? Give examples of funny words and pictures from the story.

4. What do you think life is like for Mrs. Brown now that she lives in the barn?

5. **Connecting/Comparing** What do you think would happen if Mrs. Brown's animals moved in with Maya and Julius?

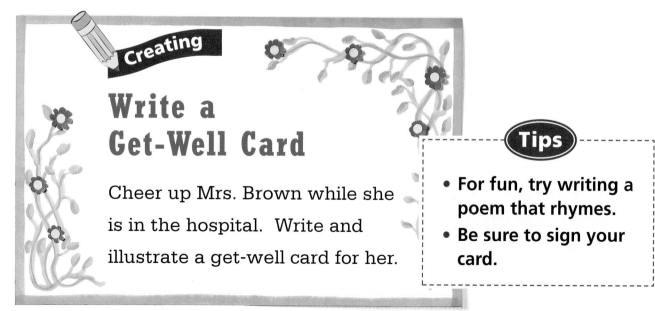

Creating

Write a Get-Well Card

Cheer up Mrs. Brown while she is in the hospital. Write and illustrate a get-well card for her.

Tips

- For fun, try writing a poem that rhymes.
- Be sure to sign your card.

Math

Write a Number Sentence

Eight animals voted on whether to move into Mrs. Brown's house. One animal voted not to move into the house. How many animals voted to move into the house? Write a number sentence to solve the problem.

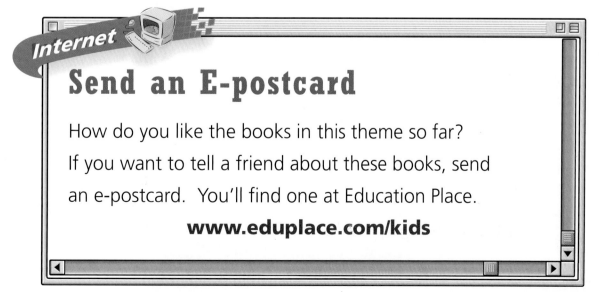

Science

Compare Animals

Copy the chart below on a piece of paper. What body parts does each animal have? Put check marks where they belong.

Send an E-postcard

How do you like the books in this theme so far? If you want to tell a friend about these books, send an e-postcard. You'll find one at Education Place.

www.eduplace.com/kids

Language Arts Link

Genre

Riddles

Skill: How to Read a Riddle

❶ Read the riddle question first.

❷ Try to guess the answer.

❸ Now read the printed answer to see if you were right.

Oodles of Riddles

1

Why should you not tell pigs secrets?

Because pigs are squealers.

Blab! Blab!

2

What do you call a cow wearing a crown?

A dairy queen.

3

Where do sheep get their hair cut?

At the baa-baa shop.

4

Where do cows go on dates?

To the moo-vies.

5

Why did the duck cross the road?

The chicken was on vacation.

6

What did the cow wear on a cruise?

A moomoo.

93

Check Your Progress

You read three very silly stories in this theme. Which one made you smile the most? Now you will read and compare two more selections and practice some test-taking skills.

On pages 13–14, Wong Herbert Yee gives you his recipe for a silly story. What things might be in a recipe for one of the stories you just read?

The next two selections are both about hippos. As you read, think about what makes the hippos silly.

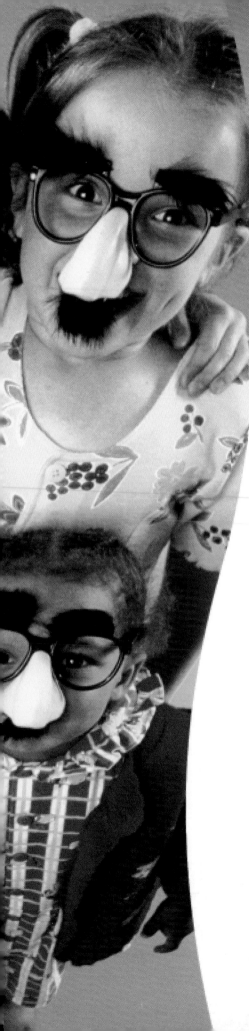

Read and Compare

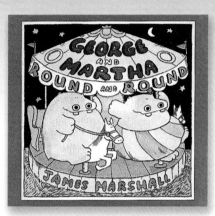

Fantasy

Find out if two friends will start talking to each other again.

Try these strategies:
Predict and Infer
Compare and Contrast

Nonfiction

Learn interesting facts about what hippos do and where they live.

Try these strategies:
Question
Evaluate

Strategies in Action *Remember to put all your reading strategies to work as you read.*

THE SURPRISE

written and illustrated by James Marshall

One late summer morning
George had a wicked idea.
"I shouldn't," he said.
"I really shouldn't."
But he just couldn't help himself.
"Here comes the rain!" he cried.

"Egads!" screamed Martha.
Martha was thoroughly drenched
and as mad as a wet hen.
"That did it!" she said.
"We are no longer on speaking terms!"
"I was only horsing around,"
said George.
But Martha was unmoved.

The next morning, Martha read a funny story.
"I can't wait to tell George," she said.
Then she remembered that she and George
were no longer on speaking terms.

Around noon Martha heard a joke on the radio.
"George will love this one," she said.
But she and George weren't speaking.

In the afternoon Martha observed
the first autumn leaf fall to the ground.
"Autumn is George's favorite season," she said.
Another leaf came swirling down.
"That does it," said Martha.

Martha went straight to George's house.
"I forgive you," she said.
George was delighted to be back
on speaking terms.
"Good friends just can't stay cross
for long," said George.
"You can say that again,"
said Martha.
And together they watched the
autumn arrive.

But when summer rolled around again,
Martha was ready and waiting.

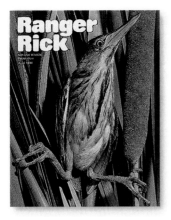

Hippos

by Claire Miller

The Big Guys

Common hippopotamuses are the third-heaviest kind of land mammal in the world. They weigh in right after elephants and rhinos.

River Horse

The word "hippopotamus" means "river horse" in the Greek language. Hippos live in big herds and eat grass, the way horses do. But they aren't close relatives of horses. In fact, hippopotamuses look and act more like pigs, which *are* their relatives.

Moving Along

When hippos are in a hurry, they can move fast on land and in shallow water. In deep water, they like to sink to the bottom. There they trot along, digging their feet into the mud.

Hippos can close their nostrils and hold their breath for about ten minutes. They aren't great swimmers, but they can "dog paddle" through the water.

A hippo's nose, eyes, and ears are on the top of its head. That way it can still breathe, see, and hear when most of its head is hidden under the water.

Daytime Soakers

You wouldn't want to watch an all-day movie on hippos. They often look like lazy lumps in the water. But resting in water is just what they have to do. They need the moisture to keep their skin from drying out in the hot sun.

What will the hippos do when dry weather turns their lakes and rivers into a mess of mud? They'll squish around and cover themselves from nose to tail. The mud becomes a sunscreen and keeps their skin wet.

Think and Compare

1. How are George and Martha in *The Surprise* like the real hippos in *Hippos*? How are they different?

2. How is *Hippos* different from the other selections in this theme? Tell two ways.

3. Who is a better friend, Martha or Maya in *Julius*? Why?

4. Think about one of the silly stories in this theme. What silly thing might happen next in that story?

Strategies in Action Tell about one or two places in *Hippos* where you used reading strategies.

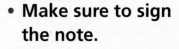

Write a Thank-You Note

Expressing

What if Dragon had a party and invited all the animals from the theme? Write a thank-you note to Dragon from one of the animals. Tell why the party was fun.

Tips

- Start the note with *Dear Dragon,*
- Make sure to sign the note.

Taking Tests

✓ Choosing the Best Answer

Some test questions have three or four answer choices. You have to choose the best answer. A test about *George and Martha Round and Round* might have this question.

Read the question. Fill in the circle next to the best answer.

1   What is the first thing Martha does after George sprays water on her?

   ○ Martha hears a joke.

   ○ Martha reads a funny story.

   ● Martha stops talking to George.

 Understand the question.

Find the key words in the question. Use them to understand what you need to do.

> I think the key words are **Martha, after,** and **water.** I need to find the answer that tells what Martha does after she gets wet.

Look back at the selection.

Think about where to find the answer. You may need to look in more than one place.

> I will find the part of the story where George sprays water on Martha. Then I will find what Martha does next.

 Narrow the choices. Then choose the best answer.

Read each answer choice. Which choices are wrong? Have a good reason for choosing an answer.

> The first two choices are wrong. Martha does not do those things until the next day. The third answer is the best choice.

Poetry

Words in a poem are
superwords. Just a few of
them can be more powerful
than you ever imagined!

What does a poem do?
A poem **describes** things, tells a **story**,
or makes you **feel** a certain way.

How does a poem sound?
A poem may have words that **rhyme**
or make a **rhythm**, like beats in music.

What does a poem look like?
A poem may have parts called **stanzas**,
or it may form a special **shape**.

Now turn the page to see and hear
what poems can do!

Contents

People..113
by Charlotte Zolotow

Covers..113
by Nikki Giovanni

Why Is It?..114
by Shel Silverstein

Migration/Migración..115
by Alma Flor Ada

Camel..116
by Langston Hughes

The Gecko..116
by Douglas Florian

There was a sad pig with a tail......................117
by Arnold Lobel

The Pickety Fence..118
by David McCord

Fish..119
by Mary Ann Hoberman

I Like It When It's Mizzly................................120
by Aileen Fisher

Wind/Viento..121
by Francisco X. Alarcón

Rest here..121
by Issa

People

Some people talk and talk
and never say a thing.
Some people look at you
and birds begin to sing.

Some people laugh and laugh
and yet you want to cry.
Some people touch your hand
and music fills the sky.

by Charlotte Zolotow

Covers

Glass covers windows
    to keep the cold away
Clouds cover the sky
    to make a rainy day

Nighttime covers
    all the things that creep
Blankets cover me
    when I'm asleep

by Nikki Giovanni

Why Is It?

Why is it some mornings
Your clothes just don't fit?
Your pants are too short
To bend over or sit,
Your sleeves are too long
And your hat is too tight —
Why is it some mornings
Your clothes don't feel right?

by Shel Silverstein

Migration

Do you know why the leaves fall
From the trees?
Maybe they want
To fly south,
Like the birds.

Migración

¿Sabes por qué se caen las hojas
de los árboles?
¿Será que quieren irse
volando al sur,
como los pájaros?

by Alma Flor Ada

There was a camel
Who had two humps.
He thought in his youth
They were wisdom bumps.

Then he learned
They were nothing but humps —
And ever since he's
Been in the dumps.

by Langston Hughes

The Gecko

by Douglas Florian

Across the ceiling it may roam,
But don't you try this in your home.
Like glue it sticks and rarely falls.
The gecko's trick is climbing walls.

There was a sad pig with a tail
Not curly, but straight as a nail.
So he ate simply oodles
Of pretzels and noodles,
Which put a fine twist to his tail.

by Arnold Lobel

The Pickety Fence

The pickety fence
The pickety fence
Give it a lick it's
The pickety fence
Give it a lick it's
A clickety fence
Give it a lick it's
A lickety fence
Give it a lick
Give it a lick
Give it a lick
With a rickety stick
Pickety
Pickety
Pickety
Pick

by David McCord

Fish

Look at them flit
Lickety-split
Wiggling
Swiggling
Swerving
Curving
Hurrying
Scurrying
Chasing
Racing
Whizzing
Whisking
Flying
Frisking
Tearing around
With a leap and a bound
But none of them making the tiniest
tiniest
tiniest
tiniest
sound.

by Mary Ann Hoberman

I Like It When It's Mizzly

I like it when it's mizzly
and just a little drizzly
so everything looks far away
and make-believe and frizzly.

I like it when it's foggy
and sounding very froggy.
I even like it when it rains
on streets and weepy windowpanes
and catkins in the poplar tree
and *me*.

by Aileen Fisher

Wind   Viento

at night   de noche
you make   tú haces
trees   susurrar
whisper   a los árboles

by Francisco X. Alarcón

Rest here
   sleepy butterfly,
   I'll lend you my lap.

by Issa

Think About the
POETRY

1. "Gecko" and "Fish" are both about animals. How are the poems alike? How are they different?

2. Compare "Why Is It?" and "There was a sad pig with a tail." Which poem do you think is funnier? Why?

3. Aileen Fisher describes what she sees in "I Like It When It's Mizzly." What do you think she hears and feels?

4. Which poem is your favorite? Why?

Internet

Take an Online Poll

What kinds of poems do you like best? Do you like poems that rhyme? Do you like shape poems? Visit Education Place and take an online poll.

www.eduplace.com/kids

Creating

Write a Poem

Write a poem. It's easy and fun to do! You can write a poem about almost anything, such as something in nature, a favorite place, or even a person. Choose your topic. Decide if you want your poem to rhyme. Will it have a special shape?

Tips

- Draw a picture of your topic. Then brainstorm interesting words that describe how your topic looks, smells, sounds, and feels.
- Read your poem aloud to hear how it sounds.
- Write a title for your poem.

2

NATURE WALK

I'm Glad

I'm glad the sky is painted blue,

And the earth is painted green,

With such a lot of nice fresh air

All sandwiched in between.

Anonymous

NATURE WALK

with Jane Yolen

Everyone in my family is a nature lover. We go on long walks together and watch animals and birds through our binoculars. We have learned to identify wildflowers and trees.

In this theme, you can become part of my family and go on a Nature Walk, too. This nature walk, though, is a reading nature walk. You won't need binoculars, only your book.

Maybe, like me, you can send postcards about your nature walks — real or reading — to friends.

126

Dear Girls and Boys,

Today I walked in a piney wood. The trees cast dark jagged shadows. I tried to call down an owl, but none answered me. I'll try again tonight. I did see two rabbits on the trail and a gray squirrel.

Your book friend,

Jane Yolen

Boys and Girls
_____
Your School
_____
Your City and State
_____

Hello Girls and Boys,

   Here is a lovely lake I visited. The water was so clear, I could almost see right down to the bottom of the lake. A fish leaped up from the water and flipped its silvery tail, making circles within circles in the water.

   Your book friend,

   Janell Johen

Boys and Girls

Your School

Your City and State

   I hope you enjoy your nature walks as much as I do. Nature walks take quiet and patience if you are to really see creatures in the wild. You are about to go on your reading nature walk in this theme. I know you will find wonderful things ahead, but you will need quiet and patience as you read, too.

Go On a Nature Walk

The postcards from Jane Yolen show you some of her favorite places. Which nature walk reminds you of a walk you have taken?

Now you will take some reading nature walks. As you read, think about how these places are the same and different. Decide which place you might want to visit!

Internet

To learn about the authors in this theme, visit Education Place. **www.eduplace.com/kids**

Henry and Mudge
and the Starry Night

HENRY AND MUDGE
AND THE
Starry Night
Story by Cynthia Rylant
Pictures by Suçie Stevenson

Genre   **Realistic
Fiction**

Key Vocabulary

backpack
campfire
camping
lantern
tent

Vocabulary Reader

Let's Go Camping

e • Glossary

Camping and Hiking

In the story you are going to read, a family goes **camping** and hiking. Have you ever gone camping in the woods? Have you ever climbed a hill? Spending time outdoors can be a lot of fun.

◀ You can carry what you need in a **backpack**.

▶ You can cook over a **campfire**.

▼ A **lantern** is a light you can use outdoors.

▲ A **tent** protects you from rain, wind, or hot sunshine.

Cynthia Rylant

Where she lives: Eugene, Oregon

How she got the idea for Henry and Mudge: When her son was seven, they met a "big, drooly dog" named Mudge.

Fun fact: Her dog Leia is pictured in Dav Pilkey's book, *Dogzilla*.

Other books by Cynthia Rylant:
Mr. Putter and Tabby Toot the Horn
Poppleton and Friends
The Relatives Came

Meet the Illustrator

Suçie Stevenson

Where she lives: By the sea on Cape Cod in Massachusetts

Pets: She has two Labrador retriever dogs that sleep under her desk while she works. If she ever forgets how Mudge would act, she just looks under her desk.

Internet

To find out more about Cynthia Rylant and Suçie Stevenson, visit Education Place.

www.eduplace.com/kids

HENRY AND MUDGE
AND THE
Starry Night

Story by Cynthia Rylant
Pictures by Suçie Stevenson

Strategy Focus

Henry and Mudge find a lot to do while they are camping. As you read, think of **questions** that you might ask about their camping trip.

Big Bear Lake

In August Henry and Henry's big dog Mudge
always went camping. They went with Henry's
parents.

Henry's mother had been a Camp Fire Girl, so she knew all about camping. She knew how to set up a tent. She knew how to build a campfire. She knew how to cook camp food.

Henry's dad didn't know anything about camping.
He just came with a guitar and a smile.

Henry and Mudge loved camping. This year they
were going to Big Bear Lake, and Henry couldn't wait.

"We'll see deer, Mudge," Henry said. Mudge
wagged.

"We'll see raccoons," said Henry. Mudge
shook Henry's hand.

"We might even see a *bear*," Henry said.

Henry was not so sure he wanted to see a bear.
He shivered and put an arm around Mudge.

Mudge gave a big, slow, *loud* yawn. He drooled
on Henry's foot.

Henry giggled. "No bear will get *us*, Mudge,"
Henry said. "We're too *slippery!*"

A Good Smelly Hike

Henry and Mudge and Henry's parents drove to Big Bear Lake. They parked the car and got ready to hike.

Everyone had a backpack, even Mudge. (His had lots of crackers.)

Henry's mother said, "Let's go!" And off
they went.

They walked and walked and climbed and
climbed. It was beautiful.

Henry saw a fish jump straight out of a
stream. He saw a doe and her fawn. He saw
waterfalls and a rainbow.

Mudge didn't see much of anything. He was
smelling. Mudge loved to hike and smell.

He smelled a raccoon from yesterday. He smelled a deer from last night. He smelled an oatmeal cookie from Henry's back pocket.

"Mudge!" Henry laughed, giving Mudge the cookie.

Finally Henry's mother picked a good place to camp.
Henry's parents set up the tent. Henry unpacked
the food and pans and lanterns. Mudge unpacked a
ham sandwich.

Finally the camp was almost ready. It needed just one more thing:

"Who knows the words to 'Love Me Tender'?" said Henry's father with a smile, pulling out his guitar. Henry looked at Mudge and groaned.

149

Green Dreams

It was a beautiful night. Henry and Henry's parents lay on their backs by the fire and looked at the sky.

Henry didn't know there were so many stars in the sky.

"There's the Big Dipper," said Henry's mother.

"There's the Little Dipper," said Henry.

"There's E. T.," said Henry's dad.

Mudge wasn't looking at stars. He was chewing on a log. He couldn't get logs this good at home. Mudge loved camping.

Henry's father sang one more sappy
love song, then everyone went inside the
tent to sleep.

Henry's father and mother snuggled. Henry
and Mudge snuggled.

It was as quiet as quiet could be. Everyone slept
safe and sound and there were no bears, no scares.
Just the clean smell of trees . . . and wonderful
green dreams.

Think About the Selection

1. Why does Henry love camping? Why does Mudge love camping?

2. What might have happened if the family had seen a bear while camping?

3. Is it a good idea to take a dog on a camping trip? Explain.

4. What would have been different about Henry's trip if it had rained the whole time?

5. **Connecting/Comparing** If you were to go on a nature walk with Henry and Mudge, what would you enjoy most?

Reflecting

Write a Journal Entry

Choose a character from the story: Henry, his mom or dad, or even Mudge. Write a journal entry about the camping trip from that character's point of view.

Tips

- **Make a list of what took place on the trip.**
- **Tell what happened first, next, and last.**

Make a Map

Henry saw hills and other land forms while hiking. Draw a map of Big Bear Lake. Label some of the land forms Henry saw.

Bonus Write a short description of each land form.

Make a Camping Catalog

Make a catalog of things campers use. Draw or cut out pictures of items such as a tent or a backpack. Label each picture.

Internet

Do a Web Mystery Grid

To find a surprise from the camping trip, print a mystery grid from Education Place.

www.eduplace.com/kids

CAMPFIRE GAMES

by Jane Drake and Ann Love

Telephone

Everyone sits in a circle around or near the fire. One person starts the game by whispering a message in the ear of the person on her right. She might say a tongue twister or something simple, such as "Dad cooks great burgers" or "Mary mixes marvelous milk shakes."

The message is passed from ear to ear until the last person repeats what he's been told. You'll be in stitches when you hear "Cool Dad eats bridges" or "Mash mealy muffins, Mary."

Campfire Telephone

Everyone sitting in the campfire circle joins hands. The person with a birthday closest to July 1 starts the game by squeezing a message to the person seated on his right. It can be an ordinary squeeze, or a series of squeezes like Morse code.

The message travels around the circle until it comes back to the start. See how much the message changes. Try to do it quickly so that the message flashes around the circle in the shortest time possible.

Rainmaker

If it's been a hot day and you need cooling off, try rainmaking. One person begins and is joined by the person on her right and so on until the action travels all the way around the circle.

The noise gets louder as each person in the circle joins in. Then the first person will do the next action and it will travel around the circle.

Round 1

Rub your hands together so they make a swishing noise.

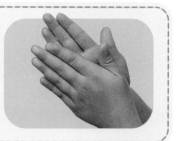

Round 2

Snap the fingers of both hands, moving your arms up and down, while making a popping sound with your tongue on the roof of your mouth. It sounds like water falling to the ground.

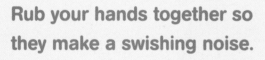

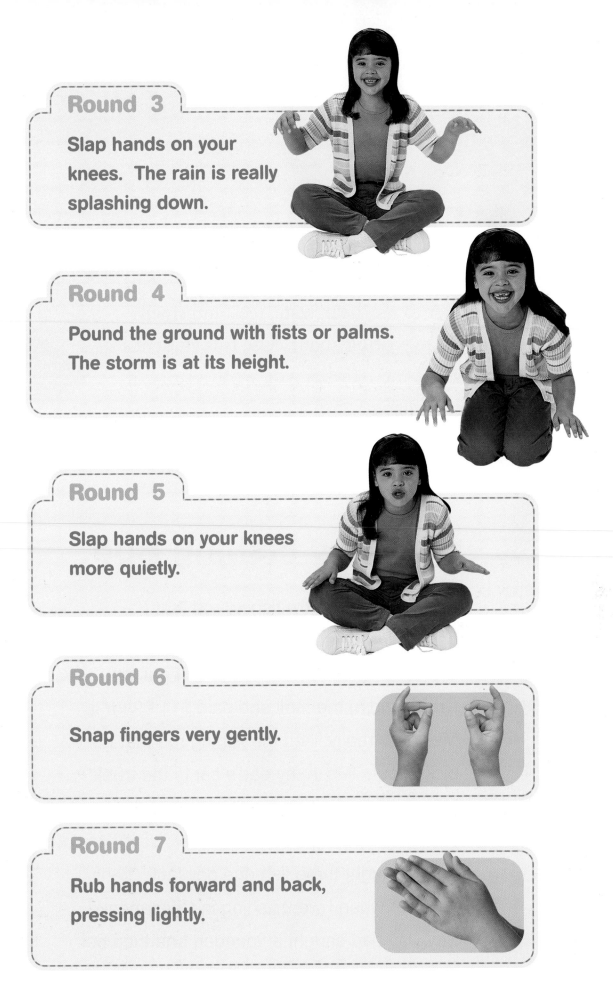

Round 3

Slap hands on your knees. The rain is really splashing down.

Round 4

Pound the ground with fists or palms. The storm is at its height.

Round 5

Slap hands on your knees more quietly.

Round 6

Snap fingers very gently.

Round 7

Rub hands forward and back, pressing lightly.

A Description

A description is a picture in words that helps the reader to see, hear, taste, feel, and smell what you're writing about. Use this student's writing as a model when you write a story of your own.

A good **beginning** tells what the description is about.

A good description includes **sense words**.

My New Fishing Rod

I bought a new fishing rod that I haven't used yet. It is red and black with white string and a black handle. I got my fishing rod at the mall and paid $11.99 for it. My father really liked the fishing rod that I picked out. It is in my dad's car in the trunk in back of the car where I'll keep it until summer. Then I can use it a lot.

I caught three fish one day last summer when I went fishing in Chesapeake Bay. My dad caught a flounder, and then he caught an oyster cracker. A flounder is as flat as a stone. The oyster cracker that my dad caught was covered with spots. I couldn't believe how ugly it was!

After fishing, we took the fish home, cleaned them, and then we ate them. Once we finished eating the fish, we went to bed. We had a fantastic time fishing.

I cannot wait to use my new fishing rod. I'll be glad when it is hot. Then I can go fishing and catch all kinds of fish like catfish, rockfish, perch, and flounder.

Telling what happened is a good way to make a description interesting to the reader.

Giving **specific names** for what you've been describing makes a good ending.

Meet the Author

Robert C.

Grade: two

State: Delaware

Hobbies: reading, Boy Scouts, fishing

What he'd like to be when he grows up: worker in the field of marine wildlife

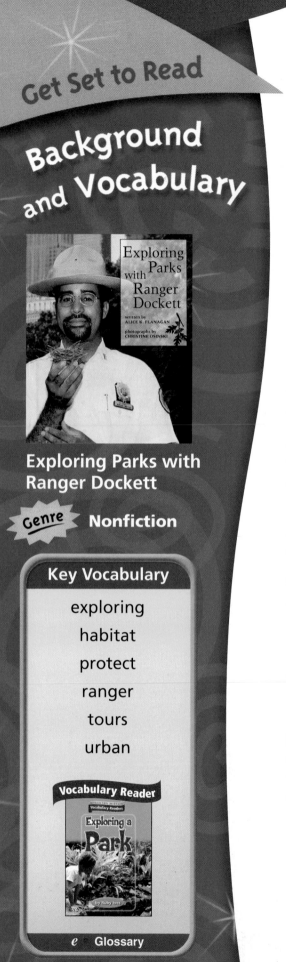

Exploring Parks with Ranger Dockett

Genre **Nonfiction**

Key Vocabulary

exploring

habitat

protect

ranger

tours

urban

Vocabulary Reader

e ▸ **Glossary**

Park Rangers

What does a park **ranger** do? Rangers care for and **protect** the plants and animals in their parks. They teach people about nature.

There are different kinds of rangers. Some are **urban** rangers who work in city parks. Others work in forests and national parks.

In the next selection, you'll learn more about what rangers do.

Rangers greet visitors at the park.

166

Rangers give **tours** of the park.

Often, rangers help animals in their own **habitat**.

Rangers show people the animals in the park.

Exploring nature with children is a fun part of the job.

Author
Alice K. Flanagan

Photographer
Christine Osinski

Meet the Author and the Photographer

Alice Flanagan and Christine Osinski are sisters. They grew up in Chicago, Illinois. When they were children, they would make books together by writing stories and drawing pictures.

Today, they still team up to make books. Ms. Flanagan writes the words and Ms. Osinski takes the photos.

Other books:

A Busy Day at Mr. Kang's Grocery Store

Dr. Kanner, Dentist with a Smile

Here Comes Mr. Eventoff with the Mail!

Internet

Visit Education Place to find out more about Alice Flanagan and Christine Osinski.

www.eduplace.com/kids

Exploring Parks with Ranger Dockett

written by
ALICE K. FLANAGAN

photographs by
CHRISTINE OSINSKI

Strategy Focus

Ranger Dockett has a busy job. As you read the selection, **evaluate** how the author helps you understand what rangers do.

Right in the middle of busy New York City is a wide, wonderful park.

It is one of many parks that Ranger Dockett takes care of as an Urban Park Ranger.

Each day, he has many tasks. He takes visitors on bird-watching walks. And he gives special tours of the parks.

Sometimes, he talks about the statues
along the paths.

There's Christopher Columbus and Alice
in Wonderland with the Mad Hatter!

On his long walks through the city parks, Ranger Dockett keeps in touch with other rangers.

Together, they make sure everyone follows the rules to keep the parks safe and clean.

Ranger Dockett does his best to make each park a safe place where people can walk or play.

Every day, Ranger Dockett teaches people
how to care for the special green spaces in the
heart of the city. He shows them how to protect
the plants and animals that live there.

Each year, he plants young trees. He explains
how important they are to the park habitat.

Sometimes, he teaches classes at the pond. He talks about the plant life at the water's edge.

His students look for turtles, frogs, and insects.

Ranger Dockett puts on special boots.
Carefully, he wades to the middle of the pond
with his net.

When he brings back mud from the bottom
of the pond, everyone searches for signs of life.
Will they find a beetle or a dragonfly?

Look! There's a snail!

Ranger Dockett was a Boy Scout when he was a little boy. Later, he went to school to learn how to be a ranger.

Ever since then, he has been exploring nature with others.

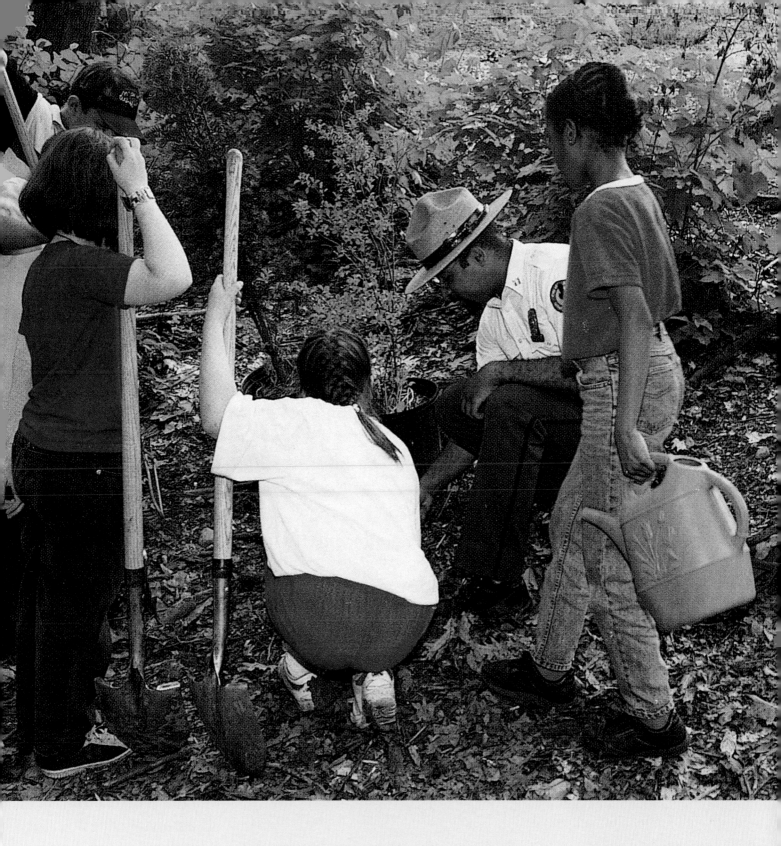

The park is his exciting classroom!

Think About the Selection

1. What did you learn about Ranger Dockett's busy job?

2. If you were a park ranger, what part of the job would you like best? Why?

3. Why is a park ranger's job important?

4. In what ways is a park like an exciting classroom?

5. **Connecting/Comparing** If Henry and Mudge were to visit Ranger Dockett's park, what would their day be like?

Informing

Write Park Rules

Ranger Dockett makes sure that everyone follows park rules. Write a list of rules for Ranger Dockett's park.

Tips

- Use command sentences, such as *Obey park rules.*

- Use words such as *always* or *never.*

184

Math

Make a Schedule

Write a list of what Ranger Dockett does in one day. Then write a time for when he might begin and end each task. Put the times in order.

Bonus Use a calculator to add the minutes for each task. Find the total number of minutes.

Listening and Speaking

Give a Talk

Role-play a visit from Ranger Dockett to your class. Plan his talk with a small group. Choose group members to be the teacher, Ranger Dockett, and the audience.

> **Tips**
> - Take turns speaking.
> - Speak clearly in a voice that can be heard.

Internet

Go on a Web Field Trip

Connect to Education Place and explore a national park or wildlife preserve.

www.eduplace.com/kids

Genre

Poetry

Skill: How to Read a Poem

- When you read a poem, try to imagine the picture that the poem describes.

- Sometimes, but not always, poems use words that **rhyme**.

- Some poems have a **rhythm**, or a pattern of beats.

Oak's Introduction

I've been wondering,
when you'd notice
me standing here.

I've been waiting,
watching you
grow taller.

I have grown too.
My branches
are strong.

Step closer.
Let's see
how high

you can

climb.

by Kristine O'Connell George

Looking Around

Bees
   own the clover,
birds
   own the sky,
rabbits,
   the meadow
   with low grass and high.

Frogs
   own the marshes,
ants
   own the ground . . .
   I hope they don't mind
   my looking around.

by Aileen Fisher

Background and Vocabulary

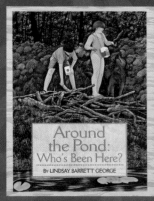

Around the Pond: Who's Been Here?

Key Vocabulary

- banks
- crater
- edge
- moss
- path
- shallow

Vocabulary Reader

At the Pond
by John Connor

e Glossary

Ponds

A pond is a body of water, smaller than a lake. In the next story, two children find many interesting animals and plants in and around a pond.

A **path** near a pond may have been made by the footsteps of animals or people.

Some fish make a small **crater** in the soil under the water to lay their eggs.

The water near the **edge** of a pond is usually not deep.

Moss and other green plants grow near the water's edge, on the **banks** of the pond.

Sometimes it is possible to see small fish and other living things in **shallow** water.

Lindsay Barrett George

Birthday: July 22

Where she was born:
The Dominican Republic

Where she lives now:
She lives in a log cabin in
Pennsylvania with her
husband and her children,
William and Campbell.

Why she wrote this book:
She spent four years living
with her family in their home
near the woods. She thought
children would enjoy reading
about the animals that were
her neighbors.

Other books:

In the Snow: Who's Been Here?
Around the World: Who's
  Been Here?

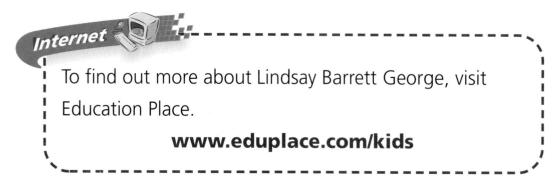

Internet

To find out more about Lindsay Barrett George, visit
Education Place.

www.eduplace.com/kids

190

Around the Pond: Who's Been Here?

By LINDSAY BARRETT GEORGE

Strategy Focus

As you read about Cammy and William's trip around the pond, **monitor** your reading. If you don't understand something, reread to **clarify** what happened.

It is warm and muggy on this summer afternoon.

"Cammy," says William, "Mom says if we pick enough blueberries, we can make a pie for dinner."

"Let's go!" says Cammy.

Cammy and her brother grab their berry containers and follow the old deer path that circles the pond.

A dead sugar maple stands alone by the water's edge.

White feathers are stuck to the bark around a hole.

Who's been here?

Two baby wood ducks

Sam finds a stick. He wants someone to throw it.

"Not now, Sam," William says. "We've got to pick blueberries."

Their dog lies down on the soft sphagnum moss.

"William, look at this footprint," says Cammy.

Who's been here?

A baby raccoon

A tree has fallen across the path and into the pond.

William dangles his feet in the water. He sees a shallow crater on the sandy bottom.

Who's been here?

A sunfish

Cammy and William reach a patch of swamp azalea. They see a pile of branches and mud.

Who's been here?

A beaver

Bits of broken shell lie on the sunny
bank. The children stop to take a closer
look.

William picks up a piece of shell.
It is soft.

Who's been here?

A painted terrapin

Cammy and her brother stop in front of a large blueberry bush. They pick and eat. Sam likes blueberries, too.

Cammy points to a long, filmy shape caught on the branches.

Who's been here?

A garter snake

Sam wades into the pond and takes a drink.

A red-winged blackbird scolds from a nearby branch. A large, gray feather floats next to a lily pad.

Who's been here?

A great blue heron

The pond is quiet and still. The late afternoon sky turns pink.

"Let's go wading," says Cammy. The mud is soft and squishy.

"Look at all the mussel shells," says William.

Who's been here?

An otter

Cammy and William reach the dock.
They have eaten most of their blueberries.

But look! Two full pails of berries are waiting for them.

Who's been here? They know!

"Come and join us,"
calls their father.
And in they go!

Think About the Selection

1. Think about the animals in this story. In what ways are they alike? How are they different?

2. Cammy and William are good nature detectives. What do you think makes a good nature detective?

3. How would this story be different if it took place in winter?

4. If Cammy and William visited Ranger Dockett's park, what clues might they find there?

5. **Connecting/Comparing** Compare Sam, the dog in this story, with Mudge. How are they alike?

Describing

Describe an Animal

Choose a picture of an animal from the story. Write a description of that animal.

Tips

- List details about the animal.
- Use adjectives to describe how the animal looks, smells, and feels.

Identify Living Things

Make a chart with three columns. Label one column **L** for *Living*. Label the second column **N** for *Non-living*. Label the third column **O** for *Once-living*. Then look at the story and group things that you find.

Look for Classroom Clues

Practice being a detective in your classroom or school. Look for clues, such as a half-eaten sandwich or a broken crayon. Ask yourself, "Who's been here?"

Tips

- Choose an area of the school or classroom to explore.
- Take notes on what you see.

Do a Web Crossword Puzzle

Test what you know about the plants and animals in *Around the Pond: Who's Been Here?* Print a crossword puzzle from Education Place.

www.eduplace.com/kids

How to Be a Wildlife Spy

From *Ranger Rick* magazine

by Carolyn Duckworth

Watching wildlife is like a sport — the more you learn and practice, the better you get at it, and the more fun you have!

Look Here, Look There

One of the neat things about spying on wildlife is that you can do it almost anywhere. Even in a car, you can look out the window and try to see hawks soaring in the sky or deer at the edge of woods.

Try Different Times

Deer, birds, and other animals are most active around sunrise and sunset. But lots of creatures are very busy in the middle of the day. At night, *look* for bats and moths and *listen* for all kinds of animals.

Think Small

You can look for insects everywhere. Examine plants closely, peek under dead tree bark, and look in streams and ponds. (Be sure to watch out for stingers and biters.)

squirrel

salamander

hawk

217

Use All Your Senses

Look around, but also remember to sniff and listen. For example, a musky odor may be the scent of a fox. And honking cries overhead may be a flock of Canada geese.

Check Animal Signs

Sometimes you can figure out where an animal has been or what it has been doing by the signs it has left. Look along a creek for the tracks of birds, beavers, and other animals. And look for places where the grass has been pressed against the ground. A deer may have rested there.

deer track

Let Someone Know

Always let an adult know where you're going and when you'll be back. Or take an adult along — adults like to have fun too.

What to Take

Powerful "eyes." Take a magnifying glass and binoculars if you have them.

Outdoor Manners

There are nice ways and not-so-nice ways to watch wildlife. Remember, you're a guest in the animals' wild homes.

▶ Leave your pets and radio at home.

▶ Don't chase animals or try to make them fly or run. And be careful not to bother them by getting too close.

Check Your Progress

In this theme, you have read about three nature walks. You have seen how important it is to notice the things around you. Next, you will read and compare two more selections and practice some test–taking skills.

Think about what Jane Yolen wrote to you on pages 126–128. How did her advice help you while you were reading?

Now get ready to read two selections about owls and where they live. As you read, notice how the owls are alike and different.

Read and Compare

Realistic Fiction

See what happens when a girl and her father look for owls on a cold winter night.

Try these strategies:
Predict and Infer
Question

Nonfiction

Learn more about what owls look like, where they live, and how they hunt for food.

Try these strategies:
Monitor and Clarify
Compare and Contrast

Strategies in Action *Always use all your reading strategies while you read.*

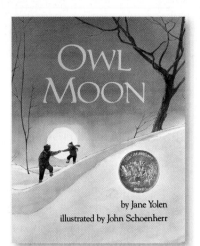

Owl Moon

by Jane Yolen
illustrated by John Schoenherr

On a cold winter night, a little girl goes owling with her father. The moon is bright, and their footsteps crunch through the snow. They don't talk. They just hope to see an owl.

We went into the woods.
The shadows
were the blackest things
I had ever seen.
They stained the white snow.
My mouth felt furry,
for the scarf over it
was wet and warm.
I didn't ask
what kinds of things
hide behind black trees
in the middle of the night.
When you go owling
you have to be brave.

Then we came to a clearing
in the dark woods.
The moon was high above us.
It seemed to fit exactly
over the center of the clearing
and the snow below it
was whiter than the milk
in a cereal bowl.

I sighed
and Pa held up his hand
at the sound.
I put my mittens
over the scarf
over my mouth
and listened hard.
And then Pa called:
"Whoo-whoo-who-who-who-whooooooo.
Whoo-whoo-who-who-who-whooooooooo."
I listened
and looked so hard
my ears hurt
and my eyes got cloudy
with the cold.
Pa raised his face
to call out again,
but before he could
open his mouth
an echo
came threading its way
through the trees.
"Whoo-whoo-who-who-who-whoooooooo."

Pa almost smiled.
Then he called back:
"Whoo-whoo-who-who-who-whoooooooo,"
just as if he
and the owl
were talking about supper
or about the woods
or the moon
or the cold.
I took my mitten
off the scarf
off my mouth,
and I almost smiled, too.

The owl's call came closer,
from high up in the trees
on the edge of the meadow.
Nothing in the meadow moved.
All of a sudden
an owl shadow,
part of the big tree shadow,
lifted off
and flew right over us.
We watched silently
with heat in our mouths,
the heat of all those words
we had not spoken.
The shadow hooted again.

Pa turned on
his big flashlight
and caught the owl
just as it was landing
on a branch.

For one minute,
three minutes,
maybe even a hundred minutes,
we stared at one another.

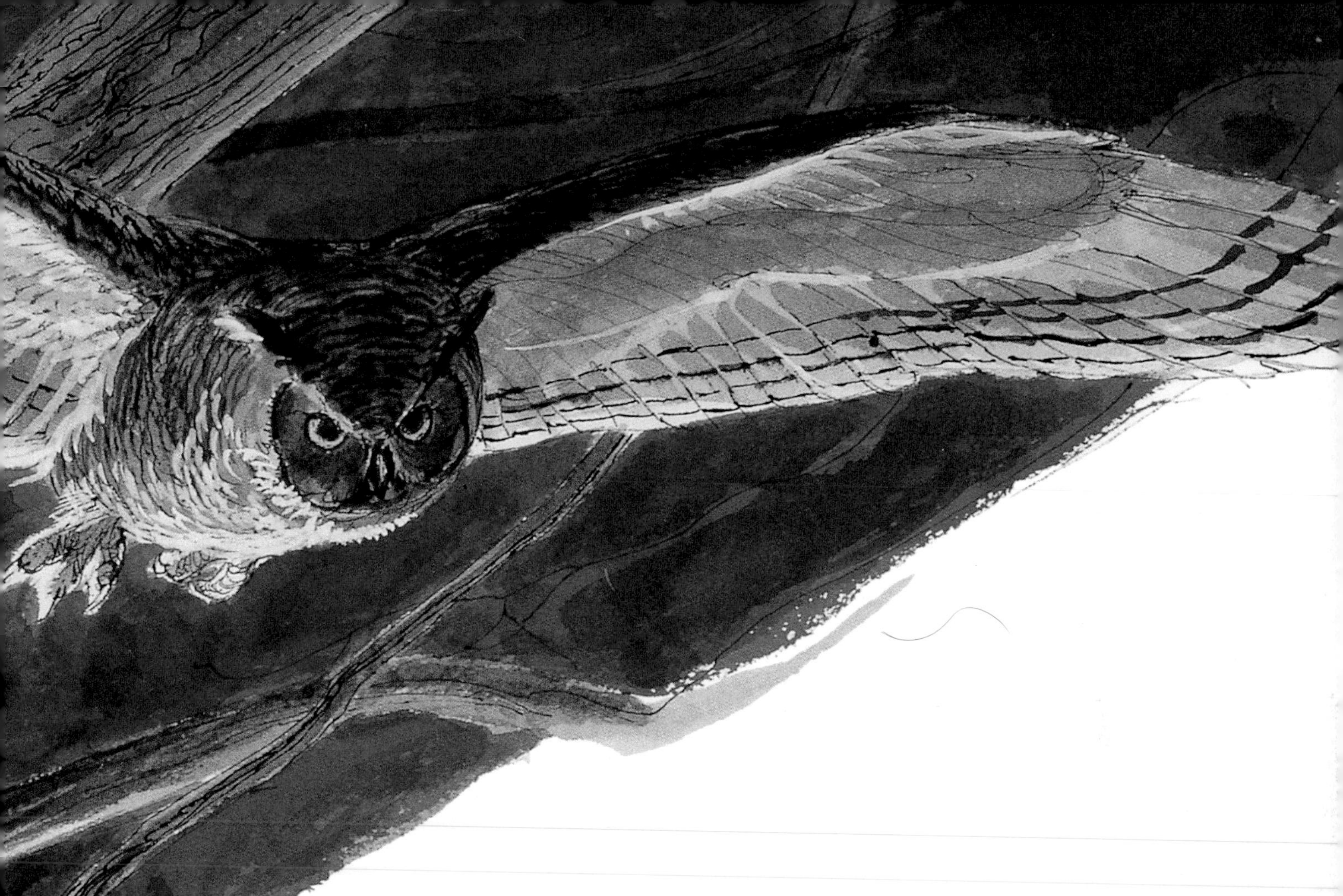

Then the owl
pumped its great wings
and lifted off the branch
like a shadow
without sound.
It flew back into the forest.
"Time to go home,"
Pa said to me.
I knew then I could talk,
I could even laugh out loud.
But I was a shadow
as we walked home.

When you go owling
you don't need words
or warm
or anything but hope.
That's what Pa says.
The kind of hope
that flies
on silent wings
under a shining
Owl Moon.

OWLS

by Michael George

People and other animals rarely see owls, even though some owls are quite large. Most owls are active at night and sleep during the day. They often sit close to tree trunks, on high branches. This resting place is called a perch. The owls' feathers blend in with the trees, making them very hard to see.

Owls look different from all other birds. They have round faces covered with soft, fluffy feathers. Their faces are outlined by two large circles called facial disks. Owls have big, round eyes. They also have sharp, curved beaks called bills.

long-eared owl

saw-whet owls

Most other birds' eyes face to the sides, but an owl's eyes face straight ahead. The owl must turn its head to see something to its side. Luckily, owls' necks bend and twist easily. An owl can turn its head so far that it can see backwards. Sometimes it looks as if its head can spin all the way around! Owls also have very good eyesight. They can even see in the dark.

barn owl

Owls use their sharp hearing and eyesight to hunt for food. Most owls hunt only at night. An owl may sit on a tree branch, watching and listening. When it spots something to eat, the owl swoops down from its perch. Soft feathers on the owl's wings help it fly very quietly.

People do not need to be afraid of owls. In fact, we should be happy that they are around. Owls hunt mice and other pests that might otherwise bother us. They also are very beautiful animals. So the next time you are in the woods at night, listen for an owl — "WHOO! WHOO!" Maybe if you hoot back, it will answer!

Think and Compare

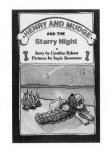

1. Compare the owls in *Owl Moon* and *Owls*. Think about what they do and where they live. How are they alike and different?

2. How is the girl in *Owl Moon* like Cammy and William in *Around the Pond*?

3. The characters in this theme use their senses to enjoy nature. Give some examples of things the characters see, hear, and touch.

4. Which of these nature walks would you like to go on? Why?

Strategies in Action Explain how you used a reading strategy while reading one of the selections.

Write a Story

Choose two characters in the theme. Write a story about a nature walk the characters might take together.

Tips
- Use words that tell about your setting.
- Tell what happens first, next, and last.

✔ Filling in the Blank

Some tests use sentences with a blank in them. You must decide which answer choice best fills in each blank. A test about *Owl Moon* might have this kind of test sentence.

> **Read the sentence. Fill in the circle next to the best answer.**
>
> **1** When Pa shines his flashlight on the owl, the owl _____.
>
> ○ hoots at them ○ winks at them
>
> ● stares at them ○ hides from them

1 Understand the sentence.

Find the key words in the sentence. Use them to understand what you need to do.

I think the key words are **flashlight** and **owl**. I need to find out what the owl does when Pa shines the flashlight.

Look back at the selection.

Think about where to find the answer. You may need to look in more than one place.

> I remember reading about when Pa shines the flashlight. I have to look for that sentence.

 Narrow the choices. Then choose the best answer.

Read the sentence, trying each answer choice in the blank. Which choices are wrong? Have a good reason for choosing an answer.

> The owl does not hoot, wink, or hide when Pa shines the flashlight. He stares at Pa and the girl. I think the third choice is correct.

FABLES

Fables

What can you learn from a crow? Plenty, in a fable!

A fable is a short story that teaches a **lesson**. The characters are usually animals who act and talk like people. Fables often end with a **moral**, or statement that tells the lesson.

See what you learn in the following fables.

CONTENTS

The Hare and the Tortoise.................242

The Crow and the Pitcher.................244

The Grasshopper and the Ants.......246

Belling the Cat.................................248

The Fly on the Wagon..........................250

from *More Fables of Aesop*
retold by Jack Kent

The Hare and the Tortoise

The hare teased the tortoise about being so pokey.

"I get where I'm going as surely as YOU do!" said the tortoise.

"But I get where I'm going FASTER," said the hare.

The fox suggested they run a race to settle the argument.

The hare laughed so hard at the idea that it made the tortoise angry. "I'll race you and I'll WIN!" the tortoise said.

The race had hardly begun before the speedy hare was out of sight.

The hare was so sure of himself that he lay down by the side of the path to take a short nap. The tortoise kept plodding slowly along.

The hare woke up just in time to see the tortoise cross the finish line and win the race.

Slow and steady wins the race.

The Crow and the Pitcher

A thirsty crow found a pitcher with a little water in the bottom. But he couldn't reach it.

He collected a number of pebbles.

Then he dropped them one by one into the pitcher. Each pebble raised the water a little higher.

And at last the crow could reach it and get a drink.

Little by little does the job.

245

The Grasshopper and the Ants

All summer long, the grasshopper sat in the sunshine and sang, while the ants were busily gathering food for the winter.

Winter came and the hungry grasshopper asked the ants for a bite to eat.

But the ants sent him away, saying, "If you were foolish enough to sing all the summer, you must dance supperless to bed in the winter."

You can't play all the time.

Belling the Cat

The mice held a meeting to decide what to do to protect themselves from the cat.

One mouse suggested that they tie a bell around his neck so they could hear him coming.

"Belling the cat is a good idea," one old mouse said . . . "but which of us is going to do it?"

Some things are easier said than done.

The Fly on the Wagon

A farm wagon rumbled down a dirt road, stirring up clouds of dust.

A fly that was sitting in the back of the wagon said, "My, my! We're raising a lot of dust, aren't we?"

*We sometimes take credit for
more than we do.*

Think About the
FABLES

1. Compare the characters in these fables. Which character is the smartest? Explain your answer.

2. What advice would you give to a character in one of the fables?

3. Why is a fable a good way to teach a lesson?

4. Think about the morals in the fables. Which moral is most helpful to you? Why?

Internet

E-mail a Friend

You have just finished reading some fables. Which fable was your favorite? Was there any fable you didn't like? Send an e-mail to a friend. Tell your friend about the fables.

www.eduplace.com/kids

Write a Fable

Think of a lesson that people can use in school or in their everyday lives. Your lesson can be a simple statement that talks about working hard, being fair, or even just telling the truth.

Read several fables to get an idea of how the story helps to explain the lesson. Then write your own fable.

Tips

- **Write a title that will get a reader's attention.**
- **List the animals and objects that will appear in your fable.**
- **Think of a moral for your fable, or choose one from the examples given.**

Morals

Little friends may become great friends.

No one believes liars, even when they tell the truth.

It's easy to dislike what you can't have.

Around Town

Neighborhood and Community

A Neighborhood Is a Friendly Place

A neighborhood is
   a friendly place.
A neighborhood is
   a friendly place.
You can say hi
   to friends passing by.
A neighborhood is
   a friendly place.

by Ella Jenkins

Around Town

with Gary Soto

Hello Friends,

In this theme, you will read about different kinds of neighborhoods. Let me tell you about the neighborhood I lived in when I was a boy. You can check my map to see where everything is.

My house was on Thomas Street. Johnny Wise lived across the street from me. We played marbles in his driveway. Johnny usually won.

Kathy Weldon lived across the street from me, too. She had a tree house. I was scared to climb up there. But one day I got brave and climbed without looking down.

Two houses down the street lived a girl with freckles and red hair. Her family had an apricot tree in their yard. The girl was always eating apricots, so we called her Apricot!

My Neighborhood

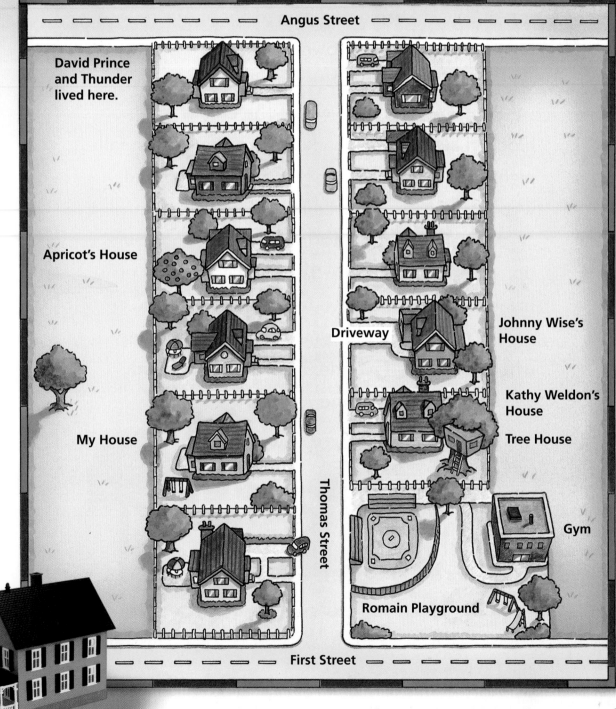

Angus Street

David Prince and Thunder lived here.

Apricot's House

My House

Thomas Street

Driveway

Johnny Wise's House

Kathy Weldon's House

Tree House

Gym

Romain Playground

First Street

257

My good friend David Prince also lived down the street. He had a dog named Thunder who was friends with my dog, Brownie. On hot days, the dogs drank water from the same bowl.

Romain Playground was at the end of my block. I liked playing basketball in the gym on fall nights. I played with Light John, a school friend who would grow up to be really big.

My neighborhood was a great place to grow up. At the end of every day, I had grass stains on my jeans from every lawn in the neighborhood.

Let's visit some other neighborhoods and see who lives there. I wonder if the neighborhoods will be like yours or mine.

Bye for now,

Gary Soto

Meet New Neighbors

Gary Soto had several good friends in his neighborhood. They played together a lot. How is his neighborhood like yours?

In this theme, you will visit six different neighborhoods. As you read, think about how the people in the selections show that they are good neighbors. Now turn the page to start your neighborhood visits.

Internet

To learn about the authors in this theme, visit Education Place. **www.eduplace.com/kids**

Chinatown

Genre **Realistic Fiction**

Key Vocabulary

apartment
delivery
handcarts
markets

Vocabulary Reader

Chinese New Year
by Bob Arrigo

e ● Glossary

What Is a Chinatown?

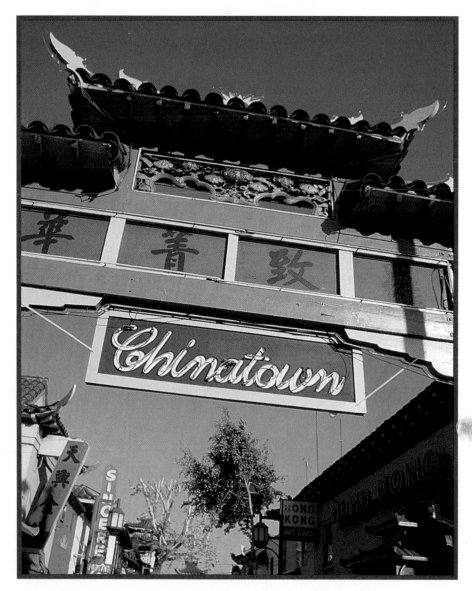

Chinatown is a name used to describe a neighborhood found in some big cities, such as New York City. Many of the people who live and work in Chinatown are Chinese Americans. You'll find out more about Chinatown in the story you're going to read next.

Chinatowns are busy places filled with **apartment** buildings, shops, restaurants, and outdoor **markets**.

Shoppers share the streets with **delivery** trucks, workers pushing **handcarts**, and even bicycles.

CHINATOWN

WILLIAM LOW

Strategy Focus

Every morning, a boy and his grandmother go for a walk in Chinatown. As you read, stop and **summarize** the important parts of the selection.

I live in Chinatown with my mother, father, and grandmother. Our apartment is above the Chinese American grocery store.

Every morning Grandma and I go
for a walk through Chinatown. We hold
hands before we cross the street. "Watch out
for cars, Grandma," I tell her.

Most days the tai chi (tie CHEE) class has already begun by the time we get to the park. Students, young and old, move in the sunlight like graceful dancers.

We always stop and say hello to Mr. Wong, the street cobbler. If our shoes need fixing, Mr. Wong can do the job. "Just like new, and at a good price, too," says Mr. Wong.

270

Chinatown really wakes up when the delivery trucks arrive. Men with handcarts move quickly over the sidewalks and into the stores.

Every day Grandma and I walk past the Dai-Dai (DYE-dye) Restaurant. Roasted chicken is my favorite, but Grandma likes duck best.

When it gets cold outside and Grandma needs to make medicinal soup, we visit the herbal shop. Inside it is dark and smells musty. The owner, Mr. Chung, is bagging dried roots and herbs.

"Winter is here," says Grandma. "We must get our strength up."

Sometimes Grandma and I go for lunch at a seafood restaurant. I like to watch the fish swim in the tank. Grandma says, "You won't find fresher fish than those in Chinatown."

The kitchen in the restaurant is a noisy place. Hot oil sizzles, vegetables crackle, and woks clang and bang. The cooks shout to be heard.

At the outdoor market I can barely move. But we go there because Grandma likes to buy fresh snapping crabs for dinner. When the crabs seem furious, Grandma is pleased. "The angrier the crabs, the tastier the meat," she says.

277

On Saturdays I take lessons at the kung fu school. Master Leung teaches us a new move each week. "To develop your body *and* your mind," says Master Leung, "you must practice every day."

My favorite holiday is Chinese New Year.
During the celebrations the streets of
Chinatown are always crowded. "Be sure
to stay close by," Grandma says.

On New Year's Day the older kids from my kung fu school march to the beat of thumping drums. Grandma and I try to find a good place to watch, and I tell her that next year I'll be marching, too.

The New Year's Day parade winds noisily through the streets. "Look, Grandma!" I say. "Here comes the lion."

Firecrackers explode when the lion dance is over. I turn to Grandma, take her hand, and say, "*Gung hay fat choy*, Grandma."

She smiles at me. "And a happy new year to you, too."

Meet the Author and Illustrator
William Low

William Low was born in the Bronx neighborhood of New York City. As a child, he liked to read comics and draw. His neighborhood became one of his favorite things to draw.

Today, Mr. Low works in his studio and teaches art at the New York School of Visual Arts. When he is not painting, he likes to go for walks with his wife, Margaret, and their dog, Sam.

Other books illustrated by William Low:

Good Morning, City
by Elaine Moore
Lily by Abigail Thomas

Internet

If you'd like to learn more about William Low and his artwork, visit Education Place.

www.eduplace.com/kids

Think About the Selection

1. How does the boy in the story feel about his neighborhood?

2. What does he learn from his grandmother?

3. If you visited Chinatown, what would you most like to see for yourself? Why?

4. What words does the author use to describe how things in Chinatown look, smell, sound, feel, and taste?

5. **Connecting/Comparing** Compare some of the jobs and businesses in *Chinatown* with those in your own community.

Describing

Describe Your Favorite Restaurant

The boy in *Chinatown* likes eating at restaurants. Describe your own favorite restaurant.

> **Tips**
>
> - Write a title for your description.
> - Use adjectives to add details to your writing.

Identify Healthful Activities

The characters in *Chinatown* do things to help them stay healthy. Explain how these activities are healthful.

Bonus **Keep a log of all the healthful activities you do during one day.**

Make Street Sounds

In a small group, think of the different sounds you might hear in Chinatown. Draw pictures of things that make sounds, such as clanging pans. Write words that stand for the sounds. Take turns holding up your pictures and making the sounds.

Internet

Post a Review

Would you recommend the book *Chinatown* to someone? Why or why not? Post a review on Education Place. **www.eduplace.com/kids**

Make a Tangram

by Margaret Kenda and Phyllis S. Williams

With most puzzles, you can put the pieces together in only one right way. With a *tangram*, you can put the pieces together in hundreds of ways.

The tangram idea comes from China. The first book to mention tangrams was published there in 1813, but the idea may be much older. No one really knows. That's part of the mystery of the tangram.

The seven pieces of a real tangram are called *tans*.

To make a tangram, use construction paper, posterboard, or other heavy paper. You may even want to cut out the tangram pieces in different colors.

Here's how to cut a square into the seven tans of a tangram:

 Begin with a square.

2. Cut the square into two large triangles.

3. Fold one of these triangles in half, and cut it along the dashed line as shown.

4. Fold the point of the other large triangle as shown and cut along the fold.

5. Fold the larger piece in half, and cut it into two pieces.

6. Fold one of the small pieces, and cut it along the dashed line as shown.

7. Fold the other small piece, and cut it as shown.

Now, see if you can put the tans together to form a square.

Play with a Tangram

Were you able to put the square back together again? Here's how to do it.

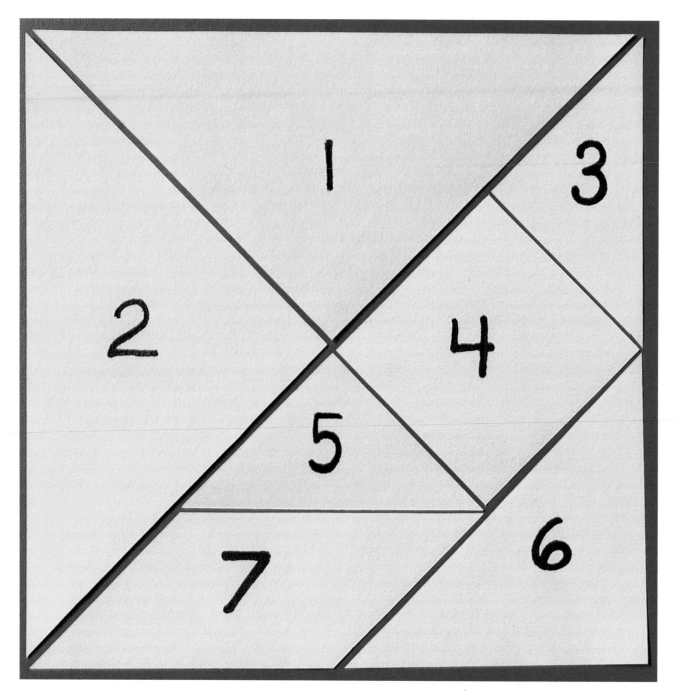

The seven pieces are numbered, so you can see where they go.

You can create your own tangram designs, or you can put together designs that other people have invented. The only rule is that you have to use all seven tans.

Here are some designs to try.

A bird flying   **A person running**   **A sailboat**

Answers for Tangrams

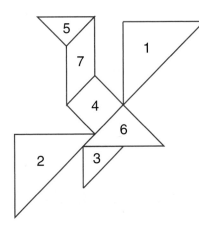

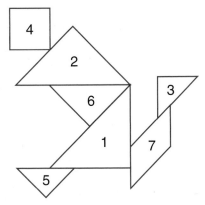

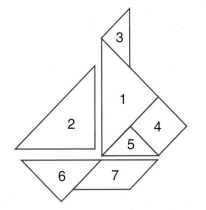

A Friendly Letter

A friendly letter tells a special friend about what you are doing. Use this student's writing as a model when you write a friendly letter of your own.

November 8, 2001

A friendly letter includes a **date**.

A friendly letter has a **greeting**.

Dear Hazel,

I wonder how you are doing. I am doing fine. My apartment is much bigger, including my room. I have a friend already. She is nice. My friend's name is Kate, and she asked me to go to her house. She has a big sister. They gave me something called blondies that were really good.

The main part of the letter is the **body**.

I have another new friend. Her name is Kacy. Kacy and I are buds at afterschool. We work together at homework club.

My teacher is nice. Afterschool art is fun.
It's too bad Kate won't go to afterschool. We
have had a lot of birthdays. I love my new school,
and I like my new apartment too.

Love,
Gaby

Adding **details** makes the letter come alive to the reader.

A friendly letter has a **closing** and the **name** of the writer.

Meet the Author

Gabriela M.
Grade: two
State: Massachusetts
Hobbies: reading, movies, arts and crafts
What she'd like to be when she grows up: a comedian and an artist

Background and Vocabulary

A Trip to the Firehouse

Genre Nonfiction

Key Vocabulary

dispatch

emergency

fire engine

firefighters

gear

Vocabulary Reader

We Are Firefighters

e ● Glossary

Fighting Fires

When a fire happens, every second counts!

At the firehouse, an alarm rings. In the **dispatch** room, an operator tells the **firefighters** exactly where the fire is.

Firefighters quickly put on their special **gear**. They climb onto the **fire engine** and speed away. They're off to take care of an **emergency**!

Learn more about firehouses and fighting fires by reading *A Trip to the Firehouse*.

294

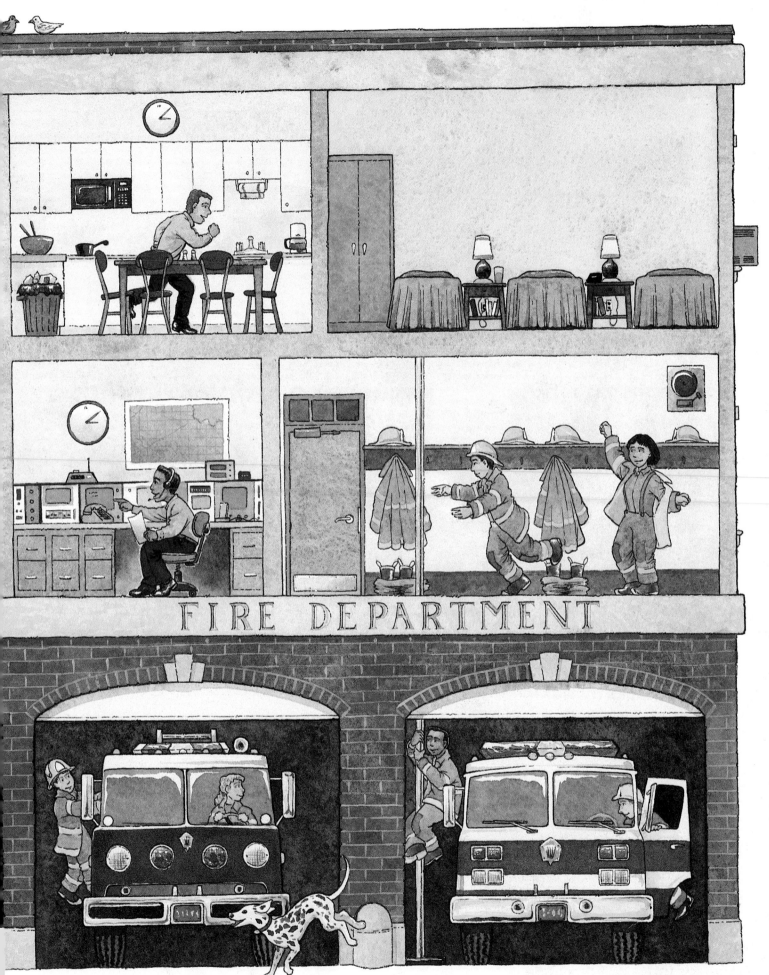

FIRE DEPARTMENT

Meet the Author

Wendy Cheyette Lewison

Where she was born:
Brooklyn, New York

Other jobs she has had:
Kindergarten teacher;
editor of children's books
and magazines

Her family: She has a husband,
John, and two grown children,
Elizabeth and David.

Other books by Wendy Lewison:
Going to Sleep on the Farm
Hello, Snow!
Buzz Said the Bee

Meet the Photographer

Elizabeth Hathon

Where she lives: On Cape Cod
in Massachusetts, with her
husband and two children

Where she works:
She owns her own photography
business in New York City.

**Other books photographed by
Elizabeth Hathon:**
I Am a Flower Girl
    by Wendy Cheyette Lewison
Daddy and Me
    by Catherine Daly-Weir

Internet

If you want to find out more about the author
and photographer, visit Education Place.

www.eduplace.com/kids

A TRIP to the FIREHOUSE

FOAM UNIT   FALMOUTH

By Wendy Cheyette Lewison
Photographs by Elizabeth Hathon

Strategy Focus

Some children are visiting their neighborhood firehouse. As you read about their visit, think of **questions** to ask about firehouses and firefighters.

David and his class are visiting their neighborhood firehouse today. That's why David is wearing a special shirt. It's fire-engine red!

The fire chief himself greets the children at the door. "Welcome to our firehouse, girls and boys," he says. "We have lots of exciting things to show you."

He lets everyone try on a real fire helmet.

Next they meet the firehouse dog. The children
guess his name. They guess right — it's Spot!

The firefighters tell them that Spot has not eaten
his breakfast yet. Would they like to come inside and
feed him? YES, they would!

While Spot is eating, the children look around.

David sees the firefighters' gear on one wall.

Three firefighters show how long it takes for them to

put it all on. Less than thirty seconds!

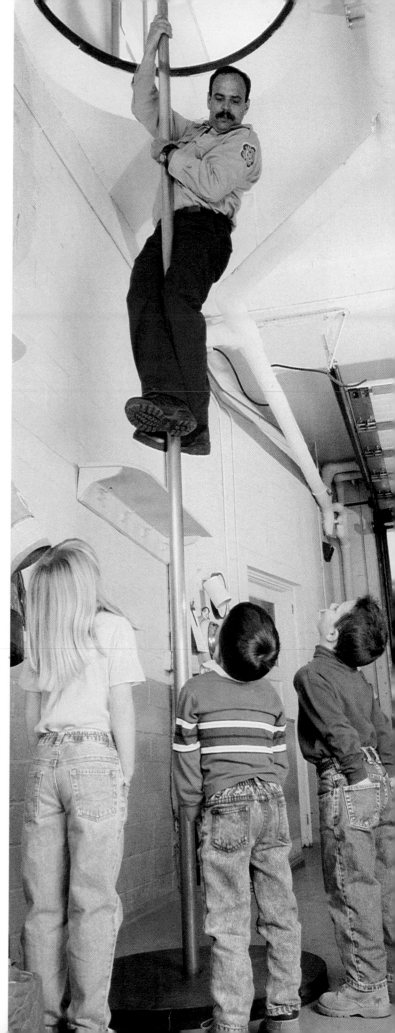

Katelyn finds the firehouse pole. "Hello-o-o, down there!" calls a firefighter way up at the top. He grabs the pole with his hands and legs, and slides down — *whoosh!*

302

The pole is an important part of the firehouse, he explains. It helps the firefighters move fast when the alarm rings. It is much faster than going down steps. When there's a fire, every second counts!

Josh points to the hole in the ceiling. "What's up there?" he wants to know.

"You can see for yourself," says the firefighter.
He leads the children upstairs.

They see where the firefighters sleep. There's a bed, a lamp, and a locker for clothes. There's even a bed for Spot.

There's a kitchen, too, where the firefighters can make themselves something to eat — and maybe share exciting stories when things are slow.

Next the children are taken to see the dispatch room. Things are never slow here!

It is busy all day and all night. Computer monitors flash. Telephone switchboards ring. It is here that phone calls come in, telling operators where the fires are.

Some calls come from 911, the number many communities use for emergencies.

It is here also that alarms come in.

An operator shows the children how the system works. Someone spots a fire and pulls a lever on an alarm box. That makes this bell clang — right here in the firehouse!

The bell clangs a certain number of times, in a pattern or code. The code is punched out on this tape, so it can be seen and recorded.

The operators look up the code on this big blackboard to find out which alarm box the alarm is coming from. Then they know exactly where to send the fire trucks.

Different kinds of fire trucks do different things. Some help at forest fires. Some help at fires in tall buildings. They carry different kinds of special equipment.

Many of these fire trucks are kept at other firehouses. But all are in perfect condition, ready to go, whenever and wherever they are needed.

Aerial Ladder Truck

Ambulance

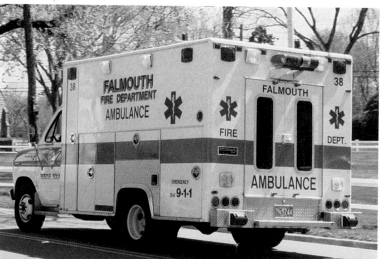

Brush Breaker

Heavy-Duty
Rescue Truck

Dive/Water Rescue Truck

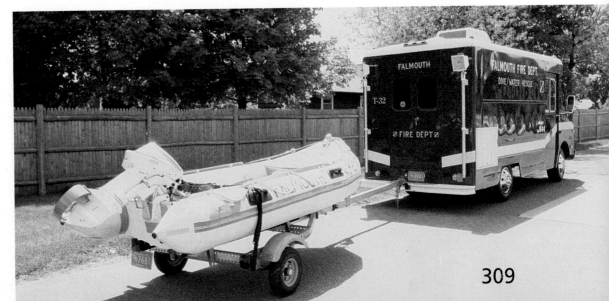

The children go downstairs now to get a good look at a fire truck that is kept at this firehouse. They climb all over it, outside and inside.

They pretend they are real firefighters, steering the big engine down the streets of town and calling the dispatch room on the two-way radio.

They examine the bell that clangs, the siren that screams, the hoses that whoosh, the valves that click.

Everything needs to be kept in perfect working order. All the parts need to be checked, and checked again.

The fire truck needs to be clean, too. And since it's such a nice day today, the children are invited to help. They soap it up and rinse it off.

Everyone has fun. Spot has fun, too, playing ball with one of the firefighters!

When the children are done with the washing,
they help a firefighter roll up a long, flat fire hose.
Katelyn thinks it looks just like a snail!

Then the rolled-up hose is stored on the truck
with other hoses — ready to use at a fire.

The firefighters tell the children they've done a great job. They deserve a special treat — bagels and cream cheese in the firehouse kitchen! Yum!

The firefighters and the children are just finishing up their snack, when — *clang! clang!* — the alarm rings!

In a flash, all the firefighters get up and rush out of the room.

Down the pole! Into their gear!

The children watch out the window while the firefighters scramble onto the fire engine.

Off they go down the street. *Whoo-ee! Whoo-ee!*

The children wave. They are sorry their visit to the firehouse is over. But they know the firefighters have a big job to do.

They hope this fire can be put out fast. And most of all, the children hope they are invited back to the firehouse soon!

Think About the Selection

1. Why do things in the firehouse need to be kept in perfect working order?

2. What do you think is the most difficult part of being a firefighter?

3. Why do you think this selection uses photographs instead of drawings?

4. Would you like to be a firefighter when you grow up? Why or why not?

5. Connecting/Comparing How do firefighters help their communities?

Explaining

Write Questions and Answers

Think about what you've learned about firefighters and firehouses. Write five questions that visitors to a firehouse might ask. Then write an answer for each question.

Tips

- **Think of questions a firefighter could answer.**
- **End each question with a question mark.**

Estimate Time

It takes less than thirty seconds for a firefighter in the firehouse to get dressed. Think of simple activities that can be done in thirty seconds or less. Act them out with a partner. Use a clock with a second hand to time yourselves.

Vocabulary

Make a Glossary

Find words in the story that tell about firehouses. Make a list of at least five words. Then put them in ABC order. Write the meaning of each word next to the word.

Bonus Write sample sentences for your words.

Internet

Label a Web Diagram

Print a diagram of a fire truck from Education Place.

Label the parts. You can color it too!

www.eduplace.com/kids

Fire-Safety Tips

by Martin C. Grube

Talk over these fire-safety tips with your whole family. How many do they already know?

Test Your Smoke Detector

Every home should have at least one battery-operated smoke detector on every level of the home and in or near all sleeping areas. Ask a parent to test the smoke detector monthly and to replace the battery with a new one once a year.

Stop, Drop, and Roll

If your clothes catch fire, don't run. Instead, stop where you are; drop to the ground, covering your face with your hands; and roll back and forth on the ground to smother the flames.

Practice Fire Drills

Ask your parents to develop a home fire escape plan with everyone in the household. Have a home fire drill at least twice a year, so the whole family can practice what to do if there is ever a fire. Talk ahead of time about what to do. Agree on where you will all meet outside — away from the home.

Then practice the fire drill: With everyone lying in bed, someone sounds the alarm.

Get up and feel the door to see if it is hot. If it is, use your secondary exit route to escape. If the door is not hot, check the hall for heat or signs of smoke.

If you must go through smoke, crawl low on hands and knees where the air is cleaner. (To avoid dangerous gases and heat that a fire causes near the ceiling, never stand up in smoke.)

See how long it takes for everyone to meet out front at the designated spot.

Background
and Vocabulary

Big Bushy Mustache

Genre **Realistic Fiction**

Key Vocabulary

bushy

costume

disguise

handsome

mirror

mustache

Vocabulary Reader

Mardi Gras

e • Glossary

Costumes and Disguises

In the next story, a class is planning to put on a play. Actors and actresses in a play dress up to look like different characters.

This actor is dressed up to look like a **handsome** prince. The cape is part of his **costume**.

A **mustache** and **bushy** wig can be a good **disguise**.

An actress checks her make-up in a **mirror**.

Big Bushy Mustache

by Gary Soto

illustrated by Joe Cepeda

Problems start when Ricky gets a part in a school play. As you read, try to **predict** how the problems will be solved.

People always said Ricky looked just like his mother.

"He has beautiful eyes, exactly like yours, Rosa!" said Mrs. Sanchez, the crossing guard, as his mother took him to school one morning.

"Thanks!" Ricky's mother shouted, and turned a big smile on him. "Have a good day, *mi'jo* (ME-ho)." Then she gave him a kiss.

Ricky went into school frowning. He was a boy. Why didn't people say he looked like his father?

That morning his teacher, Mrs. Cortez, brought out
a large box from the closet and set it on her desk. She
took out a hat and a *sarape.* She took out a sword and
raised it toward the ceiling.

"Class, for our next unit we're going to do a play
about *Cinco de Mayo.* That's a holiday that celebrates
the Mexican victory over the French army."

Mrs. Cortez looked around the room. Her eyes settled on Ricky. "Ricky, do you want to carry the sword?"

Ricky shook his head no.

"Do you want to wear this white shirt?"
she asked.

Again Ricky shook his head no. And he shook his
head to the sombrero, the captain's hat, the purple
cape, the tiny Mexican flag.

But when Mrs. Cortez took out a big, bushy mustache, something clicked. This time Ricky nodded yes.

For the rest of the day, the class practiced their
parts. Some of the children played Mexican soldiers.
Some of the children played French soldiers.

All the while, Ricky played with his mustache. It
tickled his lip. It made him feel tough.

When school was over, Mrs. Cortez told the class to leave the costumes in their desks.

Ricky took off his mustache. But instead of leaving it behind, he put it in his pocket. He wanted to take it home. He wanted to surprise his father when he got home from work.

Maybe Mami will take a picture of us, he thought. *We could stand next to each other in front of our new car.*

After Ricky left the school, he pressed the
mustache back onto his lip. He felt grown-up.

A man on the street called out, "Hello, soldier."
Ricky passed a woman carrying groceries. She said,
"What a handsome young man."

He passed a kindergartner, who said, "Mister, would you help me tie my shoes?"

Ricky laughed and ran home. He climbed the
wooden steps, pushed open the door, and rushed into
the kitchen, where his mother was peeling apples.

"*¡Hola, Mami!*" he said. "I'm hungry."

He looked up and waited for her to say something about his big, bushy mustache.

But she only smiled and handed him a slice of apple.

"*Mi'jo*, wash your hands and help me with the apples," she said.

Ricky's smile disappeared. Didn't she notice?

"Look, Mami. Isn't my *bigote* (be-GO-teh) great?" he said, tugging at her apron.

His mother looked at him.

"*¿Bigote*? What are you talking about?"

"This one," he said. He touched his lip, but the mustache was gone! He felt around his face. It was not on his cheek. It was not on his chin. He looked down to the floor, but it wasn't there, either.

I must have lost it on the way home, Ricky thought.
Without saying anything, he ran out the front door.

He retraced his steps, eyes wide open. He dug
through a pile of raked leaves. He parted the tall grass
that grew along a fence. He looked in the street,
between parked cars, and in flower beds.

He jumped with hope when he saw a black thing.
But when he bent over to pick it up, he discovered that
it was a squashed crayon.

Ricky sat on the curb and cried. The mustache
was gone.

When he got home, Ricky told his mother what had happened. She wiped her hands on a dish towel and hugged him.

At dinner, he wanted to tell Papi too, but the words would not come out. They were stuck in his throat.

He watched his father's big, bushy mustache move up and down when he chewed.

Under his breath, Ricky whispered, "Mustache," but his father didn't hear. He talked about his work.

After dinner, Ricky went to his bedroom. With a black crayon, he colored a sheet of paper and then cut it into the shape of a mustache. He taped it to his mouth and stood before the mirror. But it didn't look real. He tore it off, crumpled it, and tossed it on the floor.

In the closet, Ricky found a can of black shoe polish. He looked in the mirror and smeared a line above his lip, but it was too flat, not thick and bushy at all.

Finally, he dug out a pair of old shoes. The strings were black. He cut them in short strips and bound them together with a rubber band. He held the creation above his lip. It looked like a black mop. And smelled like old socks.

That night, after he put on his pajamas, Ricky went
into the living room, where his father was listening to
the radio. "Papi, I lost my mustache . . .
mi bigote."

His father laughed. "What mustache?"

Ricky climbed into his father's lap and told him everything. His father smiled and told him a story about a hen that tried to become a swan. It was a good story, but it still didn't solve his problem. Tomorrow he would have to face Mrs. Cortez.

The next morning, Ricky got out of bed slowly.
He dressed slowly. He combed his hair slowly. At
breakfast, he chewed his cereal slowly. He raised his
eyes slowly when his father came into the kitchen.

Ricky pressed the new mustache to his lip.
He ate his cereal, and the mustache moved up and
down, just like his father's.

But something was different about his father's smile. His lip looked funny. Ricky jumped up and threw his arms around Papi's neck.

"*Gracias*, Papi! Thank you!" he cried.

"That's okay," Papi told him. "But next time listen to your teacher."

Then Papi touched his son's hair softly. "And, hey, now I look just like you!" Ricky grinned a mile wide.

When Ricky walked to school, he carried the
mustache not on his lip, but safely in his pocket.

It wasn't just a bushy disguise anymore, but a gift
from his papi.

Meet the Author
Gary Soto

Gary Soto grew up in Fresno, California. When he was nineteen, he thought he might like to be a writer. He has since written many books for children and adults.

Mr. Soto teaches creative writing at the University of California in Berkeley. He has produced films for children, and runs a reading program for community-college students in California.

Meet the Illustrator
Joe Cepeda

Joe Cepeda's son was born while he was working on the illustrations for *Big Bushy Mustache*. He drew his family into the illustration on page 343. That's Mr. Cepeda, his wife, and his son looking over the fence!

Some other books by Gary Soto and Joe Cepeda:
Cat's Meow
The Old Man and His Door

Internet

To read more about this fantastic book-making team, visit Education Place. **www.eduplace.com/kids**

Think About the Selection

1. How do you think Ricky felt when he realized that he'd lost the mustache?

2. What do you think Ricky learned from this experience?

3. What would you do if you lost something that belonged to your classroom?

4. What if Ricky's father had not given him his mustache? How would the story be different?

5. **Connecting/Comparing** Compare Ricky's neighborhood to the boy's neighborhood in *Chinatown*.

Expressing

Write a Dialogue

Write a dialogue between Ricky and his teacher. Have Ricky explain what happened to the mustache. You may want to role-play your dialogue with a partner.

Tips

- Look at dialogue in the story.
- Use quotation marks before and after spoken words.

Social Studies

Make a Job Toolbox

Make a list of community helpers found in the story. Pick one of the jobs, or think of another type of community helper. Find a small box to use as a toolbox. Then fill it with the things someone would need to do the job you've picked. Draw or cut out pictures of tools.

Viewing

Look at Photographs

Find photographs of men with mustaches. Look in magazines or catalogs. Look for different shapes and colors of mustaches. Then make a Mustaches poster.

Internet

E-Mail a Friend

What did you like about *Big Bushy Mustache*? What didn't you like? Send an e-mail to a friend. Tell your friend about the story.

Genre

Poetry

Skill: How to Read a Poem

- Read each line slowly and carefully.

- Read the poem more than once.

- Pay attention to punctuation.

- Read the poem aloud quietly to a classmate.

Family Poems

Sick Days

On days when I am sick in bed
My mother is so nice;
She brings me bowls of chicken soup
And ginger ale with ice.

She cuts the crusts off buttered toast
And serves it on a tray
And sits down while I eat it
And doesn't go away.

She reads my favorite books to me;
She lets me take my pick;
And everything is perfect —
Except that I am sick!

by Mary Ann Hoberman

Thinking Time

Our television's broken,
There's silence in the air,
Silence in the living room,
Silence everywhere.

It gives my brain a time to think,
My eyes a time to see —
I love this silent evening time,
Just family and me.

by Patricia Hubbell

Families, Families

FAMILIES, FAMILIES
All kinds of families.
Mommies and daddies,
Sisters and brothers,
Aunties and uncles,
    And cousins, too.

People who live with us,
People who care for us,
Grandmas and grandpas,
    And babies, brand new.

FAMILIES, FAMILIES
All kinds of families.
Coming and going,
Laughing and singing,
Caring and sharing,
    And loving you.

by Dorothy and Michael Strickland

Background and Vocabulary

Subway Travel

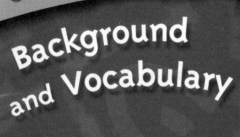

Jamaica Louise James

Realistic Fiction

Key Vocabulary

booths

stations

subway

token

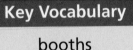

e ● Glossary

Not all trains run above the ground. In some big cities, **subway** trains go underground. They travel in tunnels all across the city.

Subway **stations** are places where subway trains stop to pick up people and drop them off. In the story you are about to read, a special event takes place inside a subway station.

Times S- 42 Stree-

A **token** is a type of coin used to pay for a trip on a subway train.

Tokens are sold in token **booths**.

Entry E F G

Meet the Author
Amy Hest

Before becoming a writer, Amy Hest was a children's librarian. "All my life, though, I secretly wanted to write children's books." Ms. Hest was born in New York City. She still lives there, less than half a block from Sheila White Samton.

Meet the Illustrator
Sheila White Samton

Sheila White Samton can see Amy Hest's building from her apartment window. "We didn't know each other before doing the book, but now we run into each other all the time."

Other books by Sheila White Samton:

*Ten Tiny Monsters: A Superbly
    Scary Story of Subtraction*
Frogs in Clogs

Internet

Would you like to learn more about the author and the illustrator of this book? Visit Education Place. **www.eduplace.com/kids**

JAMAICA LOUISE JAMES

AMY HEST

illustrated by
Sheila White Samton

Jamaica Louise makes her community a happier place. As you read, **evaluate** how well you like the story and the characters.

I was the one with the COOL idea...

368

It happened last winter and the mayor put my name on a golden plaque. It's down in the subway station at 86th and Main. You can see it if you go there.

That's me. You better believe it!
Want to hear my big idea?

I'll tell but you've got to listen to the whole story, not just a part of it. Mama says my stories go on . . . and on . . . . Whenever I'm just at the beginning of one, she tells me, "Get to the point, Jamaica!" or "Snap to it, baby!" But I like lacing up the details, this way and that.

MAMA

GRAMMY

JAMAICA
LOUISE
JAMES

This story begins with me. I have a big artist pad with one hundred big pages and five colored pencils with perfect skinny points.

Sometimes I set myself up on the top step of our building, where everyone can see me. Everything I see is something I want to draw.

373

At night, Mama and Grammy and I cuddle on the couch while the city quiets down. I show them every picture every night.

Sometimes I tell a story as I go. Sometimes they ask a question like, Why does the man's coat have triangle pockets? Other times we don't say a word.

Now look at me on birthday #8. Grammy and Mama dance around my bed. "Open your present!" they shout. "We can't wait another minute!"

Know what they did? They bought me a real paint set — with eight little tubes of color and two paint brushes. Paint sets cost a lot, I worry.

"My! My!" they say. "Are you going to spend birthday #8 WORRYING, when you can be doing something wonderful such as PAINTING THE WORLD?"

So that's when I get my BIG idea.

Now, this part of the story tells about my grammy, who leaves for work when it is still dark. Sometimes I wake up halfway when she slides out of bed. In winter she gets all layered, starting with the long-underwear layer.

She and Mama whisper in the kitchen. They drink that strong black coffee. Grammy scoops up her brown lunch bag and goes outside.

I'm scared in the night. Not Grammy. At 86th and Main she goes down . . . and down . . . into the subway station.

All day long people line up at Grammy's token booth. They give her a dollar or four quarters, and she slides a token into their hand. Then they rush off to catch the train.

Tokens
$1.00

86TH ST

380

Now, I like subways because the seats are hot pink and because they go very fast. But I don't like subway stations. Especially the one at 86th and Main. There are too many steep steps (fifty-six) and too many grownups who all look mad. The walls are old tile walls without any color.

When Grammy comes home, she sews and talks about the people she sees, like Green-Hat Lady or Gentleman with the Red Bow Tie. Mama reads and hums.

But I paint, blending all those colors until they look just right. Every day I add a picture to my collection and every day I think about my cool idea.

383

At last it's the morning of Grammy's birthday.
Mama and I get up early. We get all layered and
sneak outside. Mama holds my hand. I am scared
but also VERY EXCITED.

We swoosh along in our boots in the dark
in the snow. At 86th and Main we go down . . .

and down . . .

fifty-six steep steps.

3111

We don't buy a token at the token booth. We
don't take a ride on the subway. What we do is hang
a painting on the old tile wall. Then another. And
another . . . and one more. Before you know it, that
station is all filled up with color.

Surprise!

we shout when Grammy comes clomping down the steps.

She looks all around that station. "Jamaica Louise James," she calls, "come right here so I can give you a big hug, baby!"

JAMAICA
LOUISE
JAMES,
AGE 8

So now you know the whole story. Everyone
sure is in love with my subway station! You'd be
surprised. People are talking to each other — some
even smile. "That looks like me!" says a lady in a
green hat to a gentleman with a red bow tie.

Then Grammy tells everyone about Jamaica
Louise James, age 8.

THAT'S ME. YOU BETTER BELIEVE IT!

Think About the Selection

1. When does Jamaica Louise first think of her big idea?

2. How does Grammy feel about Jamaica Louise's big idea? How do you know?

3. Why do you think the grownups on the subway look mad?

4. Would you like to be friends with Jamaica Louise? Why or why not?

5. **Connecting/Comparing** In what ways is Jamaica Louise's grandmother like the grandmother in *Chinatown?* How are they different?

Narrating

Write a Story

Grammy tells Jamaica Louise about people at the subway station. Choose a person from the station, such as the Green-Hat Lady. Write a story about that person.

Tips

- **Think up a name for your character.**
- **List words that describe him or her.**

Draw Pictures for Your Community

Jamaica Louise draws pictures that make people smile. Draw pictures that will make people in your community smile. Think of places where you might want to put your art.

Speak to Give a Reason

Jamaica Louise's cool idea was a success. Think of a cool idea to help your community. Think of what you would say to the mayor to convince him or her that your idea will work. Practice your speech with a partner.

Internet

Make an Online Plaque

The mayor liked Jamaica Louise's big idea so much that he had her name put on a plaque. Print a plaque from Education Place. Fill it in for yourself or for someone else.

www.eduplace.com/kids

Genre

Recipes

Skill: How to Follow a Recipe

Before you begin . . .

❶ Find an adult to work with you.

❷ Read the recipe carefully.

❸ Gather the ingredients and the tools you'll need.

While you work . . .

❶ Reread each step.

❷ Follow the steps in the correct order.

Sidewalk Sticks

by Marie E. Cecchini

Here's a recipe for homemade sidewalk chalk that's as much fun to make as it is to use.

What you'll need:

8 white eggshells

4 teaspoons hot water

red, yellow, and blue food coloring

4 teaspoons flour

mortar and pestle or aluminum pie tin and medium-sized stone

small bowl

wire whisk

spatula

foil

What to do:

1. Carefully clean and dry eggshells. Place a few shells at a time in mortar and use pestle to grind into powder. Or put eggshells in pie tin and grind them with stone. It may take a few minutes to grind eggshells completely.

2. Put 1 teaspoon hot water into small bowl. Add 1 or 2 drops food coloring.

3. Add 1 teaspoon flour to water and food coloring and stir well with whisk.

4. Add 1 tablespoon eggshell powder and stir with whisk until mixture is well blended and sticky.

5. Use a spatula to scrape mixture out of bowl and into your hands. Firmly shape the mixture into a stick. Set finished stick on a piece of foil to dry. Thoroughly rinse and dry bowl.

Repeat steps 2 through 5 until you have 4 chalk sticks. Your chalk will take 2 or 3 days to dry once you've shaped it.

Check Your Progress

You have just visited four neighborhoods in this theme. What did you like best about them? Now you will read and compare two new selections and practice some test-taking skills.

Think about how Gary Soto describes his neighborhood. Which neighborhood in the theme is most like his?

Get ready to visit two other neighborhoods. As you read, think about why each place is a good neighborhood.

Read and Compare

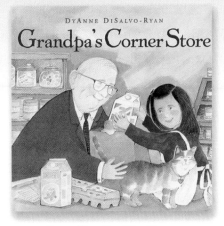

Realistic Fiction

Find out how a little girl can be a big help to her grandfather.

Try these strategies:
Monitor and Clarify
Summarize

Nonfiction

Take a walk through a boy's busy city neighborhood.

Try these strategies:
Question
Compare and Contrast

Strategies in Action *Remember to use all your reading strategies while you read.*

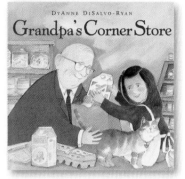

Grandpa's Corner Store

written and illustrated by DyAnne DiSalvo-Ryan

Lucy's class is making a neighborhood map. Lucy draws a picture of her grandpa's corner grocery store for the map. Her classmate Steven says that the little store will close when the big, new supermarket opens. Lucy feels sad. How can she help her grandpa?

In school on Monday, I won't even look at Steven. He keeps waving around a flyer he ripped from a pole on the avenue—

SUPERMARKET OPENS NEXT WEEK.

"I hope your grandpa likes Florida," he says, teasing. I grab the flyer out of his hand and throw it into the wastebasket.

We take turns pasting up more buildings. Somebody puts a tag with the words *mud pile* where the supermarket is being built, but Miss McCartney takes it down. I think that somebody is me.

"A community is a group of people who live and work together," Miss McCartney says, pointing to our map.

I think about what our community would be like without my grandpa's store.

And then I look at Steven and smile. Miss McCartney has given me an idea.

"Be there Saturday morning,"
I tell all the kids on my way home
after school.

"Nine o'clock sharp,"
the firefighters say.

"I'll help spread the
word," says Mr. Tutti.

"Not a problem."
Mr. Lee sneezes.

Mrs. Kalfo pats my
arm. "You can count on
me," she says.

It snows every single day that week. Clouds hang frozen in the winter sky like sheets dried stiff on a clothesline. But that doesn't stop the supermarket from opening up on Saturday. Colored flags snap in the wind. SPECIAL! SPECIAL! SALE TODAY! My mother and I yank on boots, pull down hats, and head for Grandpa's store.

"I hope this works," I tell my mother as we brave our way around the corner.

Neighbors are bunched in front of the grocery all packed up like snowballs.

"Here comes Lucy!" Chief Conley waves.

Mr. Lee is pouring out coffee. Mrs. Duffy has her five kids bundled up onto a sled.

Mrs. Kalfo is laughing. "Your grandpa can't see us. His windows are all iced up."

There's the carpenter's truck, the kids from school — even Miss McCartney's here.

I take a deep breath and push the door open.

"Where is everybody?" I ask Grandpa, trying to keep the secret.

"Probably at the supermarket," he says. "Who needs this place now?"

"You'd be surprised," I tell my grandpa.

That's when the old front door claps open, cheering for everyone as they come in. Neighbors are carrying paint cans, black and white tiles, nails and hammers, and plaster mix. Some of the people I don't even know.

"What's all this?" my grandpa asks.

"It's Lucy's idea," Mrs. Kalfo says. "We're all here to spruce up this place."

"Did you really think we'd let you get away so fast?" Chief Conley asks my grandpa.

"Who's going to make my deliveries special?" Mr. Lee wants to know.

"And what about our cheese and pickle sandwiches?" the firefighters remind Grandpa.

"And you know me," Mr. Tutti says. "I need yesterday's news today."

"Do you still want this?" I ask Grandpa, taking down the FOR SALE sign.

Grandpa looks around his store. People keep coming in left and right, banging their feet, rubbing their hands, and getting to work. Grandpa walks into the kitchen and comes out holding my colored-in grocery store.

"Thank you, Lucy," he whispers, handing it back to me. "I think your map will need this now." Then Grandpa hugs me, broom and all.

Well, the grand opening of the new supermarket was a huge success. Steven was right. The supermarket is big. But it isn't bigger than a whole neighborhood.

In school Steven pastes a big rectangle on our map and marks it "supermarket."

I raise my hand. "Bigger but not better," I tell Miss McCartney. Then I paste my grandpa's grocery store right around the corner from my house. Milk, juice, butter, eggs — it has everything you need close by. And best of all, it has Grandpa.

BARRIO

José's Neighborhood

written and photographed by George Ancona

José Luís is eight years old and lives in San Francisco, California. In his neighborhood, many people speak both English and Spanish. José's neighborhood is called *El barrio* (BA-ree-o).

José Luís lives in the barrio and goes to the Cesar Chavez (SEH-zar CHA-vez) Elementary School. On the back of the school, a new mural is being painted. The mural is the work of artists who have also painted many other buildings in the barrio. The murals of the barrio sing out the stories of the neighborhood.

Carnaval (car-nah-VAHL) is the biggest fiesta (fee-ES-ta) in the barrio and is celebrated in the spring. It brings together the people of the barrio for a weekend of music, dance, and a parade. On Sunday everyone joins the parade. The students and teachers wear bird costumes with wings and feathers. Children from barrio schools and people of many cultures march in the parade.

One street is closed to traffic for several blocks, and food stands, rides, and two stages have been set up. The delicious smells of tacos, barbecue, dumplings, gyros, and many other dishes from around the world fill the air. Musicians on stages at either end of the street play music throughout the weekend.

Besides fiestas, other activities bring neighbors together. Three community gardens in the barrio keep people busy during the summer months. One borders a new playground where neighbors plant shrubbery. In another garden, parents and children plant seeds and harvest vegetables in their own individual garden plots.

Soccer is the most popular sport in the barrio. José has been playing with his neighborhood team for five years. He has won many trophies. On Saturday José's father takes him to play a match in another neighborhood. During the game his father calls out advice to José from the sidelines. José makes two goals and his team wins 3–1. Tomorrow José will watch his dad play with a grown-up team.

Living in the barrio makes it easy for José to keep many of the customs and traditions of his parents. He also learns about the different cultures of his classmates and the people in his neighborhood. For José, the barrio is more than his home — it is a window that opens onto the entire world.

Think and Compare

1. How are the neighborhoods in *Barrio: José's Neighborhood* and *Grandpa's Corner Store* alike?

2. If Jamaica Louise lived in Lucy's neighborhood, what could she do to help with Grandpa's store?

3. Think about the selections you read in this theme. What did you learn about being a good neighbor?

4. Which community in this theme would you most like to visit? Explain your answer.

Strategies in Action When did you use a reading strategy in this theme? Tell how it helped you understand your reading.

Informing

Write a Newspaper Article

Choose one of the selections in this theme. Write a newspaper article about a neighborhood event that happened in that selection.

Tips

- Write an interesting headline.
- Use details to tell about the event.

 # Writing a Personal Response

Some test questions ask you to write about your thoughts and experiences and connect them to what you have read. Here is a sample question about *Grandpa's Corner Store*.

Write your answer to this question.

How is Grandpa's corner store like a favorite place in your community?

---

1 **Understand the question.**

Find the key words. Use them to understand what you need to do. Decide what to write about.

2 **Get ready to write.**

Look back at the selection. List details that help answer the question. Think about yourself. List thoughts or experiences that answer the question.

Here is a sample planning chart.

Story Details	My Experiences
Grandpa makes cheese and pickle sandwiches.	Marvin's shop has yummy ice cream flavors.
Neighbors spend time together in the store.	I spend time with my friends at Marvin's.

Write your answer.

Use details from both of your lists. Write a complete answer.

Now look at this sample answer.

Grandpa's store is special to people in his community. Neighbors like to go there because Grandpa does nice things for them. Grandpa makes cheese and pickle sandwiches for the firefighters. He brings special deliveries to Mr. Lee.

A special place in my community is Marvin's Ice Cream Shop. I like to go there because they have lots of ice cream flavors. My mother takes me there after my soccer games. My friends from the team go there, too. We sit together and have hot fudge sundaes.

This glossary can help you find the meanings of some of the words in this book. The meanings given are the meanings of the words as they are used in the book. Sometimes a second meaning is also given.

A

apartment

One or more rooms in a house or building used as a place to live: *There are six rooms in our* ***apartment.***

B

backpack

A bag worn on the back to carry things: *My* ***backpack*** *is very heavy because it has so many things in it.*

backpack

balance

To have the correct amounts of: *We could not* ***balance*** *the teeter-totter because one end was too heavy.*

balanced

A form of **balance**: *A* ***balanced*** *meal includes many different kinds of food.*

bank

The sloping ground along the edge of a river or lake: *Many trees and bushes grow along this* ***bank*** *of the river.*

booth

A small stand where things are shown or sold: *Six people stood in line at the ticket* ***booth.***

bushy

Thick and shaggy: *The dog's hair was so* ***bushy*** *you couldn't see its eyes!*

C

camp

To stay outdoors in shelters such as tents or cabins: *My parents bought a tent because we love to camp.*

campfire

An outdoor fire used for warmth or cooking: *Angela's mother built a campfire to cook dinner.*

campfire

camping

A form of **camp**: *We packed food and other supplies for our camping trip.*

celebration

A party or other activity to honor a special day: *Birthday parties are my favorite kind of celebration.*

chief

A person who leads other people: *The chief was in charge of all the officers at the police station.*

commotion

Noisy activity; confusion: *The commotion made by people talking and laughing woke the baby.*

costume

Special clothing worn by someone in a play or dressing up like someone else: *Ana and her friends wore flower costumes to the party.*

M

market

A public place where people buy and sell goods: *Tom's father buys apples at the **market** to make pies.*

mirror

A piece of glass that you can see yourself in: *Maria looked in the **mirror** to see her new hat.*

mirror

moss

Small green or brown plants that grow close together like carpet on the ground, rocks, and trees: *Some **moss** is growing in the shady area under that tree.*

moss

mustache

The hair growing on a person's upper lip: *Whenever our teacher drinks milk, he gets some on his **mustache**.*

N

noise

One or more loud sounds: *The car horns made so much **noise** they woke me up.*

P

path

A place where you can walk through a field or forest: *The cleared **path** in the woods made walking easy.*

plaque

A flat piece of wood, metal, or stone that has words on it about a person or event: *Russell was given a **plaque** with his name on it for winning the contest.*

protect

To keep safe: *Sunglasses **protect** your eyes from bright sunlight.*

R

ranger

A person who works in and watches over a forest or park: *The park **ranger** gave my mother good directions.*

ranger

release

To set free: *I'm going to **release** the caterpillar I caught.*

released

Form of **release**: *The boy* *released the bird from the cage.*

restaurant

A place where people go to eat meals: *Instead of cooking, Mr. Chen ate dinner at a restaurant.*

S

shallow

Not deep: *We can walk along the edge of the lake, where the water is shallow.*

shop

To go to stores to look at or buy things: *We go once a week to shop for food at the grocery store.*

shopper

A person who goes to stores to look at or buy things: *Only one shopper was in the store all afternoon.*

shopping

Form of **shop**: *Jack went shopping for a new shirt.*

sign

A thing that something does that can help you learn about it: *The dog's movements were signs that it wanted to play.*

slurp

To drink or sip something noisily: *My mother doesn't like it when I slurp my soup.*

slurped

Form of **slurp**: *Nadia slurped her chocolate milkshake until it was all gone.*

spread

To open out wide or wider: *The painter spread old newspaper on the floor in case the paint spilled.*

station

1. A stopping place along a route for taking on and letting off passengers: *We got off at the wrong* **station** *and had to wait for another train.*

2. A place or building where community helpers work: *The fire trucks drove into the fire* **station**.

station

subway

A train that travels through underground tunnels: *Mrs. Sanders takes the* **subway** *to and from work everyday.*

T

tent

A place to sleep when you camp, usually made of cloth and held up with poles: *Sheila taught Robbie how to set up his* **tent** *at the camp.*

tent

tire

To make or become weak from work or effort: *Our legs began to* **tire** *from the long walk home.*

token

A piece of stamped metal that is used instead of money, as on buses and subways: *We had to buy a **token** to get on the bus.*

token

tour

A brief trip through a place in order to see and learn about it: *The students enjoy going on **tours** of the new space museum.*

U

urban

Part of, about, or placed in the city: *Travis moved away from the country to live in an **urban** area.*

V

vegetable

A plant or plant part that is used as food: *I like orange **vegetables** such as carrots and sweet potatoes.*

vegetables

W

wear

To have on the body: *I think I will **wear** my new coat outside today.*

wearing

Form of **wear**: *Melissa was **wearing** a pretty red dress at the party.*

Acknowledgments

Main Literature Selections

Around the Pond: Who's Been Here?, by Lindsay Barrett George. Copyright © 1996 by Lindsay Barrett George. Reprinted by permission of HarperCollins Publishers.

Barrio: José's Neighborhood, by George Ancona. Copyright © 1998 by George Ancona. Used with permission from Harcourt, Inc.

Big Bushy Mustache, by Gary Soto, illustrated by Joe Cepeda. Text copyright © 1998 by Gary Soto. Illustrations copyright © 1998 by Joe Cepeda. Published by arrangement with Random House Children's Books a division of Random House, Inc., New York, New York.

Chinatown, text and illustrations by William Low. Copyright © 1997 by William Low. Reprinted by permission of Henry Holt and Company, LLC.

Exploring Parks with Ranger Dockett, by Alice K. Flanagan, photographs by Christine Osinski. Copyright © 1997 by Alice K. Flanagan and Christine Osinski. Reprinted by permission of Children's Press, a division of Grolier Publishing.

Selection from *Grandpa's Corner Store,* by DyAnne DiSalvo-Ryan. Copyright © 2000 by DyAnne DiSalvo-Ryan. Reprinted by permission of HarperCollins Publishers.

Henry and Mudge and the Starry Night, by Cynthia Rylant, illustrated by Suçie Stevenson. Text copyright © 1998 by Cynthia Rylant. Illustrations copyright © 1998 by Suçie Stevenson. Reprinted by permission of Simon and Schuster Books for Young Readers, Simon & Schuster Children's Publishing Division. All rights reserved.

"Hippos" is reprinted from the April 1994 issue of *Ranger Rick* magazine with the permission of the publisher, the National Wildlife Federation. Copyright © 1994 by the National Wildlife Federation.

Jamaica Louise James, by Amy Hest, illustrated by Sheila White Samton. Text copyright © 1996 by Amy Hest. Illustrations copyright © 1996 by Sheila White Samton. Reproduced by permission of Candlewick Press, Inc., Cambridge, MA.

Julius, by Angela Johnson, illustrated by Dav Pilkey. Text copyright ©1993 by Angela Johnson. Illustrations copyright © 1993 by Dav Pilkey. Reprinted by permission of Orchard Books, New York.

Mrs. Brown Went to Town, by Wong Herbert Yee. Copyright © 1996 by Wong Herbert Yee. Reprinted by permission of Houghton Mifflin Company. All rights reserved.

Selection from *Owl Moon,* by Jane Yolen, illustrated by John Schoenherr. Text copyright © 1987 by Jane Yolen. Illustrations copyright © 1987 by John Schoenherr. Reprinted by permission of Philomel Books, a division of Penguin Young Readers Group, a member of Penguin Group (USA) Inc. All rights reserved.

Selection from *Owls,* by Michael George. Copyright © 1998 The Child's World Inc. Reprinted by permission of The Child's World Inc.

"Shopping" from *Dragon Gets By,* by Dav Pilkey. Copyright © 1991 by Dav Pilkey. Reprinted by permission of Orchard Books, New York.

"The Surprise" from *George and Martha Round and Round,* by James Marshall. Copyright © 1988 by James Marshall. Reprinted by permission of Houghton Mifflin Company. All rights reserved.

A Trip to the Firehouse, by Wendy Cheyette Lewison, illustrated by Elizabeth Hathon. Text copyright © 1998 Grosset & Dunlap Inc. Illustrations copyright © 1998 by Elizabeth Hathon. Reprinted by permission of the Putnam & Grosset Group, a division of Penguin Putnam Inc.

Focus Selections

"Covers" from *Vacation Time,* by Nikki Giovanni. Text copyright © 1980 by Nikki Giovanni. Reprinted by permission of HarperCollins Publishers.

Fables in the Focus on Fables section are reprinted from *More Fables of Aesop,* retold by Jack Kent. Copyright © 1974 by Jack Kent. Reprinted by permission of June Kent.

"Fish" from *The Llama Who Had No Pajama: 100 Favorite Poems,* by Mary Ann Hoberman. Text copyright © 1959 and renewed © 1987 by Mary

by Janice VanCleave. Text copyright © 1996 by Janice VanCleave. Reprinted by permission of John Wiley & Sons, Inc.

"Sick Days" from *Fathers, Mothers, Sisters, Brothers: A Collection of Family Poems,* by Mary Ann Hoberman. Text copyright © 1991 by Mary Ann Hoberman. Reprinted by permission of Little, Brown and Company (Inc.) and the Gina Maccoby Literary Agency.

"Sidewalk Sticks," by Marie E. Cecchini from *SPIDER* magazine, July 1998, Vol. 5, No. 7. Copyright © 1998 by Carus Publishing Company. Reprinted by permission of SPIDER magazine.

"Smile" from *Bing Bang Boing,* by Douglas Florian. Copyright © 1994 by Douglas Florian. Reprinted with permission of Harcourt Inc.

"Thinking Time," by Patricia Hubbell. Copyright © 1997 by Patricia Hubbell. Used by permission of Marian Reiner for the author.

Special thanks to the following teachers whose students' compositions appear as Student Writing Models: Cheryl Claxton, Florida; Patricia Kopay, Delaware; Susana Llanes, Michigan; Joan Rubens, Delaware; Nancy Schulten, Kentucky; Linda Wallis, California

Credits

Photography

1 (t) © Trevor Pearson/Masterfile. (m) © William Whitehurst/Corbis. (b) © Philip Rostron/Masterfile. 3 © Trevor Pearson/Masterfile. 6 © William Whitehurst/Corbis. 8 © Philip Rostron/Masterfile. 10-11 (bkgd) © Stephen Simpson/Taxi/Getty Images. 11 (m) © Trevor Pearson/Masterfile. 12 Courtesy of Wong Herbert Yee. 16 (t) Artville. 18-9 (bkgd) Burke/Triolo Productions/FoodPix/Getty Images. 31 Courtesy Grolier Inc./Orchard Books. 32 (l) Eyewire. 40-1 Larry Lefever/Grant Heilman Photography 41 (tl) Larry Lefever/Grant Heilman Photography. (tr) Peter Cade/Stone/Getty Images. 42 (t) Courtesy Grolier Inc./Orchard Books. (b) Courtesy Grolier Inc./Orchard Books. 42-3 (bkgd) Alan Kearney/Taxi/Getty Images. 63 (b) ©PhotoDisc/Getty Images. 68 (l) Image Farm/ PictureQuest. (b) Peter Cade/Stone/Getty Images. 68-9 (frame) Image Farm. 69 (tl) Corbis Royalty Free. (tr) Tony Page/Stone/Getty Images. (b) Randy Wells/Stone/Getty Images. 70 Courtesy Wong Herbert Yee. 70-1 (bkgd) © Craig Tuttle/Corbis. 91 (l) ©PhotoDisc/Getty Images. 92 (t) Ron Kimball Photography. (m) Comstock KLIPS (b) Lynn M. Stone. 93 (tl) (tm) (bl) (bm) ©PhotoDisc/Getty Images. (tr) (br) Classic PIO Partners. 94-5 (bkgd) © Donna Day/Stone/Getty Images. 94 (b) © Trevor Pearson/Masterfile. 104 (b) Galen Rowell/Corbis. 105 (r) Art Wolfe/ The Image Bank/Getty Images, (l)Tom Brakefield/ Corbis. 106 Steve Bloom/Taxi/Getty Images. 115 © Dale Durfee/Stone/Getty Images. 120 © Rubberball Productions. 121 © Tony Cordoza/ Stone/Getty Images. 123 (l) © Rubberball Productions. (r) © Tony Cordoza/ Stone/Getty Images. 124-5 (bkgd) © Ted Wood/The Image Bank/Getty Images. 125 (m) © William Whitehurst/Corbis. 126 (t) Courtesy of Jason Stemple. 126–7 (border) Siede Oreis/PhotoDisc /Getty Images. 127 (b) Brian Maslyar/Index Stock Imagery, (m) Joe Atlas/Brand X Pictures/ Picturequest. 128 David Carriere/Index Stock Imagery. 131 (tl) Artville. (tr) Corbis Royalty Free. (b) Rob Walker/Workbook CO/OP Stock. 132 (t) (b) Courtesy Simon & Schuster. 132-3 (bkgd) Tim Brown/Stone/Getty Images. 159 (b) Corbis/Peter Johnson. 166 (l) ©PhotoDisc/Getty Images. (br) Corbis/Phil Schermeister. 167 (tl) Corbis/Wolfgang Kaehler. (tr) Keith Wood/ Stone/Getty Images. (bl) David Young-Wolff/ Stone/Getty Images. (br) Corbis/Jim Sugar. 168 (t) (b) Christine Osinski. (icon) ©PhotoDisc/Getty Images. 168-9 (bkgd) © Fredrik Skold/The Image Bank/Getty Images.184 ©PhotoDisc/Getty Images. 185 ©PhotoDisc/Getty Images. 188 (t) ©PhotoDisc/Getty Images. (ml) Stuart Westmorland/Stone/ Getty Images (mr) Rob Simpson/VALAN Photos. (l) PhotoTone. 189 (bkgd) Willard Clay/FPG/ Getty Images. (bl) Frank Oberle/Stone/Getty Images. (bm) John Mitchell/VALAN Photos. (br) Terry Husebye/ Stone/Getty Images. 190 Mickey Kauffman. (frame) Image Farm. 190-1 (bkgd) John R.

Bracegirdle/Taxi/Getty Images. **214** ©PhotoDisc/ Getty Images. **215** (tr) ©PhotoDisc/Getty Images. **216** ©PhotoDisc/ Getty Images. **217** (bkgd) Myrleen Cate/ IndexStock. (tl) Corbis Royalty Free. (tm) Corbis/Lynda Richardson. (tr) ©PhotoDisc/Getty Images. **218** (t) Roy Morsch/Corbis. (b) CC Lockwood/Animals Animals. **218–9** Lori Adamski Peek/Stone/Getty Images. **220-1**(bkgd) © Brownie Harris/ CORBIS. **220** (b) © William Whitehurst/Corbis. **235** (br) Alan G. Nelson Dembinsky/Photo Associates, Inc., (bl) John Warden/John Warden & Associates. **236** Stephen J. Shaluta, Jr. Dembinsky/ Photo Associates, Inc. **254-5** (bkgd) From *Look-Alikes* by Joan Steiner. Copyright © 1998 by Joan Steiner. Photography by Thomas Lindley. **255** (m) © Philip Rostron/Masterfile. **256** Corbis Images/ PictureQuest, (mr) Courtesy of Gary Soto. **260** Corbis/Nik Wheeler. **261** (t) Jan Halaska/ IndexStock. (b) Corbis/Dave G. Houser. **262** (bkgd) © Paul Kuroda/SuperStock. **285** (r) Courtesy of Henry Holt & Company. **296** (l) Courtesy Wendy Lewison. (r) Elizabeth Hathon. **296-7** (bkgd) Eric Meola/The Image Bank/Getty Images. **297–317** Elizabeth Hathon.**318** (inset) Elizabeth Hathon. (l) George Shelley/Corbis. **326** (bkgd) © Royalty-Free/Corbis. **357** (l) Carolyn Soto. (r) Michael Justice/Mercury Pictures. **365** (tl) Bud Freund/IndexStock. (tr) Comstock. (b) Jan Halaska/IndexStock. **366** (l) Michael Tamborrino/Mercury Pictures. (r) Courtesy Sheila White Samton. **366-7** (bkgd) © W. Cody/Corbis. **396-7** (bkgd) From *Look-Alikes* by Joan Steiner. Copyright © 1998 by Joan Steiner. Photography by Thomas Lindley. **396** (b) © Philip Rostron/Masterfile. **409–12** Courtesy of George Ancona, (border) Comstock Images. **416** ©PhotoDisc/Getty Images. **417** ©PhotoDisc/ Getty Images. **418** Eyewire. **419** Artville. **420** (l) Corbis Royalty Free. **421** ©PhotoDisc/Getty Images. **422** (l) ©PhotoDisc/Getty Images. (r) Photo Sphere Images/PictureQuest. **423** Corbis/ Joseph Sohm; ChromoSohm Inc. **425** (l) Corbis/ Jan Butchofsky-Houser. (r) Corbis Royalty Free.

Assignment Photography

2,16 (b), **17, 32** (r), **34, 36** (t, mb, b), **37, 64-7, 288-9, 320-2, 324-5, 394-5** © HMCo./Joel Benjamin. **109, 239, 415** © HMCo./Michael Indresano Photography **129, 287** (lr), **257-9, 291** (ml, mr), **358-9, 393** © HMCo./Ken Karp. **130, 160–3** © HMCo./Allan Landau.

Illustration

12–15 Wong Herbert Yee. **64-7** Amanda Haley. **96–103** (border) Stan Tusan. **110-11** David Diaz. **113** Jennifer Matteson. **114** Shel Silverstein. **116** Mircea Catusanu. **117** Arnold Lobel. **118-19** John Hovell. **186–7** Jui Ishida. **240-41** Normand Cousinear. **243** Craig Spearing. **245** Linda S. Wingerter. **247** Eric Brace. **249** Kumio Hagio. **251** Bernard Adnet. **257** Tom Pansini. **294-5** Brian Lies. **296** Jeff Zimmerman. **323** Lauren Scheuer. **357** Melissa Iwai. **360-1** Copyright © 2001 by Margaret Chodes-Irving. **362-3** Copyright © 2001 by Leonard Jenkins. **366, 392** Roxanna Baer.